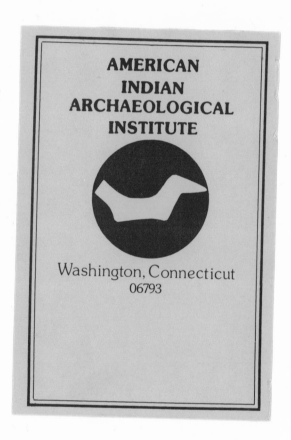

**AMERICAN
INDIAN
ARCHAEOLOGICAL
INSTITUTE**

Washington, Connecticut
06793

GREAT LAKES INDIANS

A PICTORIAL GUIDE

GREAT LAKES INDIANS

A PICTORIAL GUIDE

written and illustrated by
WILLIAM J. KUBIAK

BONANZA BOOKS • NEW YORK

The following persons and organizations are in possession of some of the paintings which were used as illustrations in this book. The author gratefully acknowledges the permission to use them in this way.

Mr. Vinson Oviatt, Potomac, Maryland, Jacket Illustration

Mr. Warren Van Ess, La Mirada, California, *Chippewa Dandy,* p. 51

Mr. Carl Adams, Grand Rapids, Michigan, *Potawatomi,* p. 144

Mr. Martin Vander Veen, Ada, Michigan, *Old Sauk Indian,* p. 155

Mr. Gerald Elliott, Grand Rapids, Michigan, *Legendary Spirit of the Sauk,* p. 159

Shrine of the Missionaries, Sault Ste. Marie, Michigan, *A Huron and Jesuit,* p. 168

Mr. Harold Yeiter, Newaygo, Michigan, *Huron War Canoe,* p. 176

Indian River Shrine, Indian River, Michigan, *Iroquois Woman,* p. 194

Mr. Lawrence O'Toole, Grand Rapids, Michigan, *Tionontati Storyteller,* p. 208

Photographs of the paintings were taken by Robert L. Kubiak.

To no one person or group can this book

be more appropriately dedicated than to

all the Indians of the Great Lakes area.

PREFACE

My first serious interest in Indians came when I met Harold Yeiter, an old friend and art associate of fifteen years. He was and still is a wonderful painter of Western Indians. Our conversations about Indians and art stimulated me enough to light the spark and ever since I have been completely fascinated by the subject. I have noticed that the more one reads and learns about the Indians, the less one feels he knows about them. It is difficult to find source material, because there just isn't that much to be found. The popular history of the Western Indians took place mainly in the nineteenth century, whereas that of the Indians in the Great Lakes area was just coming to a close at that time. The facts on Western Indians are still fairly fresh — even photographs are obtainable — but this is not true of Indians of the Great Lakes area in earlier times.

Writing and illustrating this book were somewhat like trying to put a jigsaw puzzle together, with some of the pieces missing. To get a full picture of the Indians in the Upper Midwest, one must go through scores of books, snatching a little information here and a little there, never feeling certain of what one is reading. Trying to remember the names of Indians, where they lived, and where they came from, was and still is a difficult task. It seemed almost impossible to get a clear mental picture of how they looked, because seldom, if ever, did the books or articles carry good illustrations of them.

Most persons think Indians of the past were just Indians — they all wore war bonnets, rode horses, attacked wagon trains, and lived in tipis. This extensive illusion stems largely from movies and television.

History books in our schools today seldom, if ever, devote more than one short chapter to the subject, and this usually is poorly written and illustrated. The popular opinion of the Indian has been based upon prejudice and ignorance, for students too often receive just enough information to let them know there were some red savages who inhabited North America at one time. It is to be regretted that we don't have the Indians' side of the story to compare with that of his white counterpart.

Far from being satisfied, I wanted to know what a Miami looked like, how a Potawatomi dressed, how a Huron fixed his hair, etc. What I wanted did not exist, so I decided to do something about it. Now, fifteen years later, I have written and illustrated this book on the subject. Many of the illustrations have been drawn or painted in the last several years; a number of them have been published in the *Grand Rapids Press*. The illustrations are composites of my own interpretations gained from the bits of information and notes I have collected over these years. Just as archaeologists piece together facts to authenticate their theories, I have sought to piece together what information I could gather to create my Indian illustrations.

CONTENTS

WHO ARE THE INDIANS?

Exactly who the Indians are and how they came to be on the American continents may never be known, but many theories have been suggested, some of which are inconsistent, while others seem to have genuine merit.

A few Indians would like to believe that the Mongoloid type Asian actually stems from the American Indian, a complete reversal of the most widely held theory. Such conjecture is accompanied by a total lack of evidence to be found on either of the American continents. Archaeological evidences found in Asia point to the fact that Mongoloid cultures predate that of the American Indian.

Although there may have been more than one way the Indians traveled to the Americas, popular consensus, based on scientific research, points to the probability that American Indians had their origin in northeastern Asia. After crossing from one continent to another, they scattered throughout the New World.

Undoubtedly, all of the Indians did not make this historic move at one time. Probably several, if not hundreds, of large and small migrations, stretching over many years, helped to make up the American Indian race. In some instances migrations may have been forced movements due to a conquering enemy, or by starvation and the search for new and better hunting grounds. Others may have come just because they were curious as to what lay to the east where the sun always rises.

Looking at a map, one can see there are many possibilities of crossing over from Asia to North America. The Bering Strait, approximately forty miles wide, appears to be the most logical point of crossing. The Aleutian Islands, which start at the tip of the Alaskan Peninsula, extend westward in a slightly curving line to the Kamchatka Peninsula, extending southward into the Sea of Okhotsk and the Pacific Ocean. It is interesting to note that the Chinese were aware of the Kamchatka Peninsula at a very early date in history. Of course, any migration by way of this route would involve travel from island to island. Extending southwest from Kamchatka are the Kuril Islands, a chain of islands that lead to Japan or the mainland again. A voyage following this route could have been made in a small craft by following the great thermal ocean current without much danger to the voyagers since they would have been almost within sight of land throughout the entire journey, with only a few minor exceptions.

One cannot rule out the possibility that at one time a land bridge extended between Asia and North America, thus enabling people to cross from one continent to the other with ease. It is also possible that at an early date an ice cap covered part of the Pacific Ocean, providing a crossing point not unlike that which exists in the Arctic today. Still another possibility is travel over the seas, arriving on North American shores by accident.

The time of the migration from Asia to the Americas is unknown at present, but it is generally thought to have occurred during the concluding part of the last Ice Age. A few think that the Indian may have been living in the Americas forty thousand years ago; however, at the present time there is not enough evidence to substantiate this belief. Reliable evidence indicates that Indians were living on the American continents between 9000 B.C. and 12,000 B.C.

The early prehistoric Indians who came to live in the Great Lakes area probably arrived at different times in a series of migrations that stretched over several, and in some cases, thousands of years. We actually do not know their real names, but through evidences of their cultures, archaeologists have been able to identify separate groups and have given them scientific names.

Following is a listing of the main prehistoric Indian cultures that existed in the Great Lakes area. The time spans are approximate.

PREHISTORIC INDIANS IN THE GREAT LAKES AREA

Early Archaic	8000 B.C. to 2500 B.C.
Paleo Indians	7000 B.C. to 5000 B.C.
Aqua Plano	7000 B.C. to 4500 B.C.
Borea Archaic	5000 B.C. to 500 B.C.
Old Copper	5000 B.C. to 500 B.C.
Red Ocher	1000 B.C. to 500 B.C.
Early Woodland	1000 B.C. to 100 B.C.
Hopewell	100 B.C. to A.D. 700
Upper Mississippi	A.D. 800 to A.D. 1600
Late Woodland	A.D. 800 to A.D. 1600
Middle Mississippi	A.D. 100 to A.D. 1300

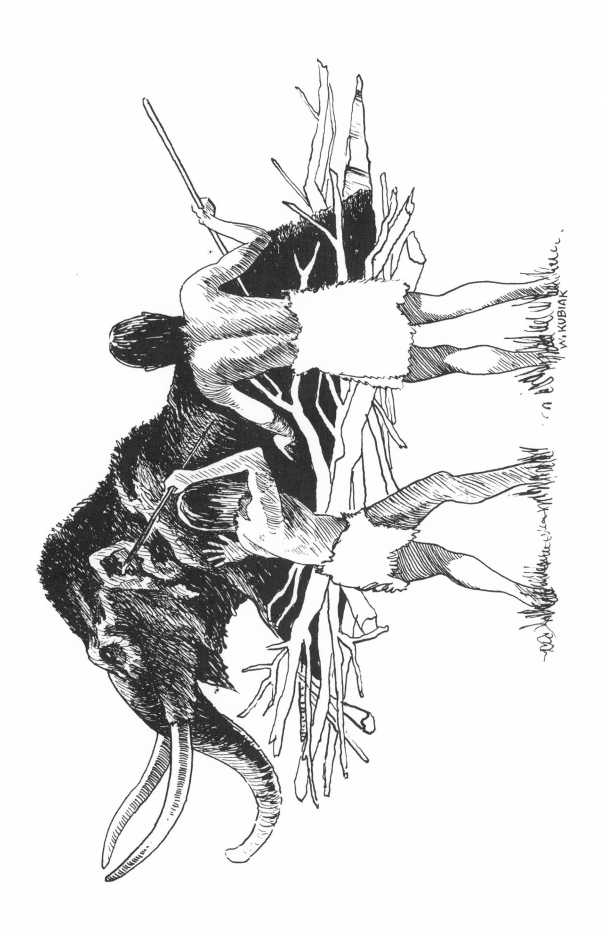

PALEO INDIANS

W. KUBIAK

The physical characteristics of the American Indian vary throughout the Americas. He differs in size, shape, color, and facial characteristics, which makes it next to impossible to find descriptive words, terms, and phrases which apply to all. They probably have their origins in several different racial stocks, of which the Mongoloid is the dominant one.

One must acknowledge the fact that the American Indians were America's first true discoverers. They were the first to see the Rocky Mountains, the Grand Canyon, the giant redwoods, the Mississippi River, the St. Lawrence River, the American prairies and plains, the Everglades, and the Great Lakes. They, and only they, should be recognized for these achievements.

There exists a narrative, recorded in Chinese history, about Hui Shen, a Buddhist missionary who, it is said, visited America during the latter part of the fifth century A.D., hundreds of years before the visits of the Norsemen or the arrival of Columbus. In this sole existing narrative America was referred to as the land of Fusang.

Early Chinese writings refer to a distant land which lay approximately sixty-five hundred miles to the east of China. It was identified as *Fusang* or in some cases *Fusu*. This land, according to these writings was about 3,250 miles across to where it runs into a large body of water or sea, which could be what we know today as the Atlantic Ocean. Hui Shen gave a detailed account of the journey through the Aleutian Islands on to Alaska, including the length of the trip and a description of the natives they met on the way. He noted particularly their ways of life — their manners and customs, their government, funerals, marriages, dress, buildings and foods — all of which correspond with the civilization of Mexico. Documentation of Hui Shen's travels is found in authentic Chinese historical documents. These records cover ancient times in America, along the Pacific shores, from Alaska to Mexico, and also farther inland. This account was considered important enough to be kept in the Imperial Archives of the Liang dynasty and is recounted with good authority by the eminent Chinese historian, Ma Tuan-Lin. During A.D. 458, five Buddhist monks visited Fusang, where they taught and spread their beliefs. They succeeded so well that they were able to ordain some of the Indian population as monks, and as a result some of the customs and manners were changed.

In Mexico there are several records which refer to visitors

BOREAL ARCHAIC INDIAN WITH SPEAR THROWER

W.KUBIAK

and teachers arriving there from the north in early times. In these narratives, written before the invention of printing, copying errors could have crept in, but surprising coincidences in the similarity of the Mexican Indian and the Asiatic civilization cannot be overlooked.

The Norsemen were, no doubt, the first Europeans to see and set foot on this continent's shores. Increasing evidence points to the fact that they reached America before Christopher Columbus, even though Columbus' great achievement is the first recorded by Europeans. In fact, the Norsemen are believed to have filtered into Minnesota territory by way of Hudson Bay, and several artifacts attributed to the Norsemen and the controversial Kensington Stone have been unearthed in these areas. This presents the possibility of an early European race, such as the Norsemen, amalgamating with the native Indians during their occupation. But again it must be emphasized that this land had already been discovered and inhabited by the Indian for thousands of years before this first European excursion.

George Catlin, the famous painter of Indians, in his letters and notes on the North American Indians, 1841, describes a small tribe of Indians, located on the west bank of the Missouri River, about eighteen hundred miles above St. Louis and approximately two hundred miles below the mouth of the Yellowstone River. He writes, "The Mandans are certainly a very interesting and pleasing people in their personal appearance and manners; differing in many respects, both in looks and customs, from all other tribes which I have seen. . . . There is certainly great justice in the remark; and so forcibly have I been struck with the peculiar ease and elegance of these people, together with the diversity of complexions, the various colours of their hair and eyes; the singularity of their language, and their peculiar and unaccountable customs, that I am fully convinced that they have sprung from some other origin than that of the other North American tribes, or that they are an amalgam of natives with some civilized race.

"Here arises a question of very great interest and importance for discussion; and, after further familiarity with their character, customs, and traditions, if I forget it not, I will eventually give it further consideration. Suffice it then, for the present, that their personal appearance alone, independent of their modes and customs, pronounces them at once, as less than savage.

MOUND BUILDER

"A stranger in the Mandan village is first struck with the different shades of complexion, and various colours of hair which he sees in a crowd about him; and is at once almost disposed to exclaim that 'these are not Indians.'

"There are a great many of these people whose complexions appear as light as half breeds; and amongst the women particularly, there are many whose skins are almost white, with the most pleasing symmetry and proportion of features; with hazel, with grey, and with blue eyes, — with mildness and sweetness of expression, and excessive modesty of demeanour, which render them exceedingly pleasing and beautiful.

"Why this diversity of complexion I cannot tell, nor can they themselves account for it. Their traditions, so far as I have yet learned them, afford us no information of their having had any knowledge of white men before the visit of Lewis and Clarke, made to their village thirty-three years ago. Since that time there have been but very few visits from white men to this place, and surely not enough to have changed the complexions and the customs of a nation. And I recollect perfectly well that Governor Clarke told me, before I started for this place, that I would find the Mandans a strange people and half white.

"The diversity in the colour of hair is also equally as great as that in the complexion; for in a numerous group of these people (and more particularly amongst the females, who never take pains to change its natural colour, as the men often do), there may be seen every shade and colour of hair that can be seen in our own country, with the exception of red or auburn, which is not to be found.

"And there is yet one more strange and unaccountable peculiarity, which can probably be seen nowhere else on earth; nor on any rational grounds accounted for, — other than it is a freak or order of Nature, for which she has not seen fit to assign a reason. There are very many, of both sexes, and of every age, from infancy to manhood and old age, with hair of a bright silvery grey; and in some instances almost perfectly white.

"This singular and eccentric appearance is much oftener seen among the women than it is with the men; for many of the latter who have it, seem ashamed of it, and artfully conceal it, by filling their hair with glue and black and red earth. The women, on the other hand, seem proud of it, and display it often in an almost incredible profusion, which spreads over their shoulders and falls as low as the knee. I have ascertained, on a careful enquiry, that about one in ten or twelve of the whole tribe are what the French call 'cheveux gris,' or greyhairs; and that this strange and unaccountable phenomenon is not the result of disease or habit; but that it is unquestionably a hereditary character which runs in families, and indicates no inequality in disposition or intellect. And by passing this hair through my hands, as I often have, I have found it uniformly to be as coarse and harsh as a horse's mane; differing materially from the hair of other colours, which amongst the Mandans, is generally as fine and as soft as silk.

"The reader will at once see, by the above facts, that there is enough upon the faces and heads of these people

EARLY DUGOUT

to stamp them peculiar, — when he meets them in the heart of this almost boundless wilderness, presenting such diversities of colour in the complexion and hair; when he knows from what he has seen, and what he has read, that all other primitive tribes known in America, are copper-coloured, with jet black hair.

"From these few facts alone, the reader will see that I am amongst a strange and interesting people, and know how to pardon me, if I lead him through a maze of novelty and mysteries to the knowledge of a strange, yet kind and hospitable, people, whose fate, like that of all their race is sealed; — whose doom is fixed to live just long enough to be

EARLY WOODLAND INDIAN AT DEADFALL

W.KUBIAK '63

imperfectly known, and then to fall before the fell disease or sword of civilizing devastation."

Catlin theorized in later notes and letters that this tribe could have been a mixture of Indian and Welsh. This was probably due to the many legendary claims about an explorer, a Welsh prince by the name of Madoc. He was supposed to have traveled over the Atlantic in about 1170 A.D. The legend has it that he colonized and settled far into the interior of the North American continent. Early English pioneers, who were moving westward to the Missouri River met Indians whom they believed to be of Welsh extraction and the survivors of Madoc's original colony. There were also Englishmen who reported coming into contact with Indians who spoke the Welsh language. The dialect was somewhat strange to them, but was recognized by them as being true Welsh. It must be remembered that Indian languages and dialects number in the hundreds and that it would not be too difficult to find similar Indian words to any language in the world even though there is no true relative connection.

From the foregoing it is obvious that no one can state with absolute certainty just who the Indians are. Some may try to present their theories as established facts, but this doesn't alter the truth that as yet there is not enough evidence to make such dogmatic pronouncements.

22

LATE WOODLAND INDIAN

INDIAN LINGUISTIC STOCK STRUCTURE

It is believed that fifty-eight totally different linguistic stocks existed north of the Mexican border. A *linguistic stock* is a family of people who speak an original language or any of the languages and dialects that were derived from it. Of the fifty-eight, three very important stocks are known to have inhabited the areas adjacent to the Great Lakes.

The first and probably the largest of all the stocks was the *Algonquian* stock. At one time the land area inhabited by members of this family of Indians was considered to be the largest of all areas occupied by North American stocks. Their "country" extended from the Rocky Mountains east to Labrador and from the uppermost part of Manitoba south to North Carolina. The name *Algonquian* is derived from the word *Algomequin,* an Algonkin word meaning "people across the river."

The second stock, probably the one most familiar to the reader, is the Iroquoian stock. The Iroquoian tribes inhabited three separate areas, all of which were separated by tribes of various other stocks. The northern region, the one with which we are concerned, was surrounded by various Algonquian tribes; those in the other regions further south did not have close association with those in the Great Lakes area. Legend says that the St. Lawrence country was formerly the territory of the Iroquoian tribes and that they progressively moved into the vicinity of the Great Lakes, where they finally settled.

Where the name *Iroquois* came from is not actually known, but some believe that it is a French adaptation of the Iroquoian words *hiro* and *koue.* Others believe it to be the Algonkin words, *irin,* meaning "real"; and *ako,* meaning "snake," with the French ending *ois.* Thus we have *Irina-kois.*

The third and least known family of Indians in the Lakes area is that of Siouan stock. This family was primarily one unit, except for a southern group that resided in Alabama and Mississippi, which was comprised of the Woccon, the Catawba, and the Tutelo. The Siouan family is believed to have migrated westward in the late prehistoric era and at one time resided in the northeast section of North America. The name *Sioux* is reputed to be a corruption of an Algonkin word *nadowessiwag,* meaning "the snake-like people," and because of this undesirable name they have been designated by many later historians as *Dakota,* meaning "friend." The name *Sioux* is used to describe the family or stock of all the tribes known to speak a Siouan dialect. The name *Dakota* is used to designate a distinct culture within the Siouan stock or family.

To simplify the above, one may consider the three stocks as being three major tribes which are made up of several smaller tribes that are separated for one reason or another. In this way one may visualize them more clearly and understand which are related.

For the convenience of the reader of this book, the three linguistic stocks have been broken down into their respective tribes of the Great Lakes area. Illustrations and maps are provided as an aid in obtaining an overall picture of how they looked, where they lived, and the articles they used. The illustrations are based upon archaeological evidence and historical accounts, although of necessity imagination plays its part in their execution. The maps represent only the general and legendary locations of the tribes at different periods. They are not meant to indicate the complete history of all movement and village sites. Because only sketchy information is available, it is impossible to draw such a map.

THEIR DWELLINGS

The villages and camp sites of Great Lakes Indians were usually located on terrain near a river, stream, or inlet, and at times along the shore of a lake. The reasons for this are obvious: they depended on the waterways as a main mode of travel and transport; such a location also provided them with a good source of food.

Three major types of dwelling were used by the Indians in the Great Lakes area: the cone-, the dome-, and the rectangular-shaped types.

The cone-shaped type was favored by most of the Algonquian tribes in winter, since it could be transported with ease and erected in a very short time. The women would search the woods for poles, which they would use to construct the framework. These poles were interlaced at the top and stuck into the ground in a circle, something like an inverted cone, so that all the poles came together directly over the center of their lodge. This is where the fire would be located, and directly above would be an opening for the smoke. On the outside of the circular framework they would place mats or bark in such a way as to shed rain or melting snow. To hold this covering in place other poles were leaned up against the covering. Around the center fireplace pine needles were spread on the ground to avoid the dampness. Over these, mats were usually spread. Sometimes the ground was dug out so that the floor of the lodge was six inches below ground level, or possibly a little more.

The Algonquians also built dome- and rectangular-shaped lodges. The dome-shaped structure was easy to transport and erect. Its shape varied somewhat, sometimes circular, but at other times oval in shape. Saplings were set in the ground in a circle to form the sides and bent so they could be twisted and locked together where they met in an arc at the top. Additional saplings were lashed horizontally around its circumference to reinforce the frame and support the rush mats or bark which was used as a covering. The majority of Algonquians used birch bark for this covering and would strip it from the trees in large pieces; however, other types of bark were also used, depending on the location. The bark of the ash, elm, spruce, and cedar were all acceptable, but birch bark and rush mats were easier to transport when on the move. These dome-shaped lodges would shelter about four Indians comfortably, depending on what one considers "comfortable."

Around the inside perimeter low benches were constructed for beds. The beds were made of sticks and brush and covered with fur or hides of animals, or mats made by the women. Directly below the hole in the dome roof the fireplace was erected. This served not only to let the smoke out, but also to let the light in.

In the summer many of the Algonquians constructed rectangular lodges or longhouses. These were much larger, providing more space per individual. They were cooler and more airy than the smaller lodges. Some of these lodges sheltered four or five families, or even more. The framework was made of saplings set in two long rows and curved at the ends. These saplings were bent or curved inward toward the middle of the lodge where they were twisted and lashed together to form an arc. More saplings were fastened horizontally, with strips of bark to strengthen the framework and provide support for the outer covering of bark sheets or rush mats, and in many cases, both. These were overlapped like roof shingles. Poles and sticks were leaned and lashed up against them to hold the sheets or mats in place. An opening, varying in width from one to two feet or more, ran the length of the lodge along the ridge of the roof. Directly underneath this long opening the fireplaces were made, the number depending on the number of families in the lodge. Usually two families, one from each side, shared a fireplace. From the ceiling poles many items were hung — food, clothing, skins, weapons, and other Indian paraphernalia.

In the latter part of the eighteenth century, the Sauk built longhouses that were constructed of neatly jointed hewn planks covered with bark so compactly that the heaviest rains could not penetrate.

The Iroquoian nations were particularly noted for their longhouses. They used them in all four seasons, with sometimes as many as twenty families in one lodge or longhouse. They were built on the same order of the Algonquian longhouses, but usually were larger. The Iroquoians used them as permanent homes. They were said to be twenty to eighty feet in length and about twenty feet in width, standing approximately fourteen feet high at the ridge or center of the longhouse. They were completely covered with bark sheets. Cedar, ash, elm, spruce, and fir bark were used, depending on the type most plentiful in the area. Only an entranceway at either end and the smoke holes in the roof were left uncovered. The ends of the Iroquoian longhouse differed from that of the Algonquian, being a flat wall all the way to the ridge. A space about twelve feet wide led from one end to the other. Down the center of this area there were fireplaces approximately eight feet apart. On both sides poles were lashed for sleeping bunks and storage bins. These were also used as benches and tables. The bedding was made of untanned skins or rush mats which the women made and decorated in various colors, by means of dyes manufactured from wild plants. The same type of mats was fastened around the walls, not only to keep out the winter chill, but also as decoration. There were no partitions in the longhouses and therefore no privacy. Groups of families lived together in these lodges, each with about eight linear feet of living space which extended about six feet from the bunks to a central fireplace. Each fireplace was shared with the family on the opposite side. These fireplaces caused the lodge to fill with smoke which floated around in lowhanging clouds, for the vent holes in the roof were not sufficiently large to allow all the smoke to escape. This caused much blindness among these Indians in their old age. Another danger was that the bark longhouses were very susceptible to fire. Many a lodge burned down in winter when the fires were kept burning steadily.

The Iroquois formerly had lodges adorned with rude wood carvings but these were burned and destroyed by the French in several raiding expeditions. When they rebuilt, they omitted the carvings. A good many Iroquoian villages were encircled by wooden palisades which afforded protection from enemies.

TYPES OF LODGES IN VARIOUS LOCATIONS

29

IROQUOIAN BARK-COVERED LONGHOUSES

30

DOME-SHAPED BARK LODGE

MAT-COVERED DOME-SHAPED LODGE

BARK-COVERED LONGHOUSE

31

MAT- AND BARK-COVERED LONGHOUSE

32

PLAINS TYPE TIPI (NOT USED IN THE GREAT LAKES AREA)

33

CONE-SHAPED BARK LODGE (POSSIBLE FORERUNNER OF PLAINS TIPI)

GABLE-TYPE LODGE

ALGONQUIAN STOCK

ALGONKIN

ALGONQUIAN STOCK

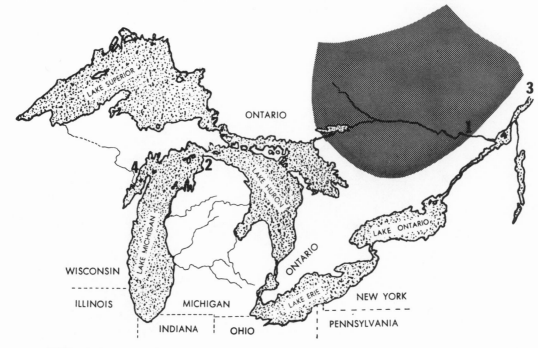

38

KEY

1. Location of the Weskarini (Algonkin) on the Gatineau River.
2. Mackinac location (consolidated as Ottawa).
3. Rendezvous point of the Algonkin tribe.

   Shaded area indicates approximate area inhabited by Algonkin Indians.

SYNONYMOUS NAMES USED IN REFERENCE TO THE ALGONKIN

Akwanake	Algonkians	Algoumequins
Algokin	Algonkins	Alkonkins
Algomeequin	Algonquians	Attenkins
Algonic Indians	Algonquins	Weskarini

ALGONKIN

The name *Algonkin* was a term originally used by the Huron and the French to identify the Weskarini Indians. The name probably implies "at the place of spearing fish and eels from the bow of a canoe." The name of the Algonquian linguistic stock was adapted from the name of this Algonkin tribe and later was applied to many other tribes speaking the same dialect or one similar to that of the Algonkin. Early French writers at various times called the Montagnais Indians, who lived in the area of the lower St. Lawrence River, the *Lower Algonquin,* because their language was similar to that of the Algonkin. The Weskarini (Algonkin) were a small tribe that inhabited the area on the Gatineau River which flows southward into the Ottawa River in what is now Quebec Province.

VERY OLD TRADE AX

The Algonkin made a close alliance with the French when they first settled in Canada and were assisted by them in defense against the Iroquois. When the Iroquois procured trade guns, they forced the Algonkin to relinquish their holdings in the St. Lawrence region. Some of the Algonkin Indians from the Ottawa River fled west to Mackinac and into other areas of Michigan where they merged (possibly with other Algonquian tribes) and became known under their present name, *Ottawa*. Some of the others retreated to the north and east to escape the wrath of the dreaded Iroquois. Later they made their way back and re-inhabited their traditional country.

There were 3,874 Algonkin Indians in Quebec Province and in eastern Ontario during 1884. This number included the Temiscaming Indians.

ALGONKIN INDIAN SPEARING

AMIKWA
ALGONQUIAN STOCK

42

KEY

1. Amikwa settlement first discovered by the French. They were located here until 1672.
2. Lake Nipissing location.
3. Probable Lake Superior location.
4. Green Bay location.
5. 1740 settlement on Manitoulin Island.

SYNONYMOUS NAMES USED IN REFERENCE TO THE AMIKWA

Amicawaes	Amikouai	Naiz Percez
Amicois	Amikouis	Nation du Castor
Amicours	Amiquoue	Nation of the Beaver
Amihouis	Beaver	Nez Perces
Amikones	Castor	Ounikanes

AMIKWA

The Amikwa (their name means "beaver") were first discovered by the French on the north shore of Georgian Bay across from Manitoulin Island. The French called them the *Nez Perces,* which means "Pierced Noses" in English. They, together with the Nipissing, once inhabited the shores of Lake Nipissing and at that time they considered themselves the dominant tribe and in control of all other Indian nations in this area.

Pierre Esprit Radisson, who inspired the organization of the Hudson Bay Company, takes note of the Amikwa in mid-seventeenth century as follows: ". . . you must note that near the Lake of the Hurons, some 40 leagues eastward, there is another lake [Lake Nipissing] belonging to the nations of the Castors [Beavers], which is 30 miles about. This nation has no other traffic nor industry than huntsmen.

NOSE RING

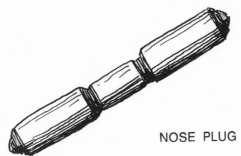

NOSE PLUG

They need to go once a year to the furthest place of the Lake of the Hurons to trade their beavers for Indian corn, for some color made of nettles, for sacks, and such things, for which they were curious enough."

They remained in control until disease struck their tribe down, thus weakening their strength and number and finally forcing them to succumb to the reign of the Iroquois. Some of the remaining Amikwa abandoned their homeland for friendly French settlements, while some went to Lake Superior and others to Green Bay. There were a small number of Amikwa that settled on Manitoulin Island in 1740. There seems to be no accurate population record but the tribe was considered small in number. It is very possible that the Nipissing and Amikwa originally were one tribe.

44

AMIKWA STALKING THEIR PREY

CHIPPEWA

ALGONQUIAN STOCK

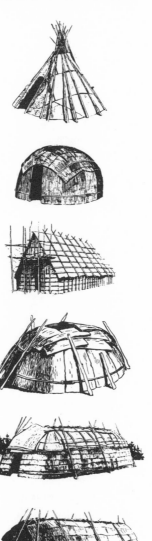

KEY

1. Approximate early legendary location.
2. Sault Ste. Marie settlement.
3. La Pointe settlement during the sixteenth century.
4. Approximate western location on Lake Superior.
    A. Bold broken lines indicate the approximate Chippewa lands in the Lakes area.

SYNONYMOUS NAMES USED IN REFERENCE TO THE CHIPPEWA

Achipoes	Chippewyans	Outchibous
Anishinabe	Dowaganhas	Pillagers
Beaver Island Indians	Jibewas	Saulteaux
Bedzaqetcha	Nation du Sault	Salteur
Bungees	Ojibwas	Sault Indians
Chipeways	Ojibays	Souteus
Chipewyans	Ostiagahoroones	Twakanha
Chippewaians	Otchipwe	Wahkahtowah
Chippewais	Ouchipawah	

CHIPPEWA

The Chippewa called themselves *Anishinabe*, which means "first man" or "original man." They were called *Ojibwa* by the neighboring Indian tribes. This name was later corrupted by the French and British into the word *Chippewa*, the name by which they are presently known. The French name for them was *Saulters*.

Legend relates that the Chippewa, Ottawa, and Potawatomi originally were one tribe that came down from the north, arriving at the upper region of Lake Huron at an early time and later dividing into three distinct tribes. The Chippewa tribe was considered to be one of the largest tribes north of Mexico and the largest subdivision of the Algonquian stock. They formed a confederacy with the Potawatomi and Ottawa which was known as the *Three Fires*.

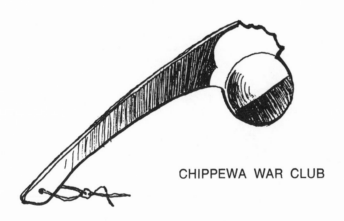

CHIPPEWA WAR CLUB

The Chippewa ranged in an area from the shores of Lake Huron, Lake Superior, and the upper part of Lake Michigan all the way across the southern part of Canada and the states of Wisconsin and Minnesota to the Turtle Mountain area in North Dakota. It is believed that from 1500 until 1612 there was a large Chippewa village at La Pointe, Wisconsin. It is also presumed that they abandoned this site at that time, some returning to Sault Ste. Marie and the remainder moving west, the largest group to the western side of Lake Superior and a small remnant moving north of Lake Superior. The Chippewa were visited at Sault Ste. Marie by Isaac Jogues and Charles Raymbault, both Jesuit missionaries, in 1642 when the Chippewa were at war with a western tribe believed to be the Sioux.

In 1692, the French established a post at La Pointe in Wisconsin, which developed into a significant Chippewa settlement. During the first part of the eighteenth century the Chippewa drove the Fox tribe from northern Wisconsin, forcing them to retreat and take refuge with the Sauk. After this the Chippewa waged war with the Sioux, driving them completely out of the territory, across the Mississippi River and westward through Minnesota to the Turtle Mountains in North Dakota.

The Chippewa participated in all the frontier wars up to the close of the War of 1812. Those who resided within the boundaries of the United States agreed to sign a treaty in 1815 and have respected it. They were all placed on reservations and allotted lands inside territory they had

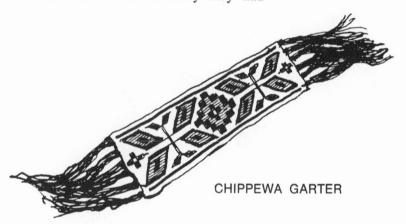

CHIPPEWA GARTER

held in Michigan, Wisconsin, Minnesota, and North Dakota. However, a small band of Black River and Swan Creek Chippewa sold all their land and moved to Franklin County, Kansas, where they are with the Munsee.

A Chippewa band residing near Lake Superior became known as *The Pillagers*. They received this name not because they were known for plundering, but because they attacked an American fur trader who was living with them, and took all his belongings. The trader had treated the Indians unfairly, yet this solitary act aroused such irate feelings among their neighbors, both European and Indian, that they were given this name.

The Pillager band practiced the custom of permitting an Indian brave who had scalped an adversary to wear two

W. KUBIAK

CHIPPEWA HUNTER

eagle feathers on his head, while if he captured his foe he gained the right to wear five feathers.

The Beaver Island Indians were a Chippewa band which formerly lived on islands by that name in the upper part of Michigan.

The Chippewa are believed to be one of the bravest tribes of the eastern Algonquian and were very strictly disciplined while on the trail. They were armed with wooden war clubs, bows and arrows, knives, and round moose- or other hide-covered shields. Their cone-shaped or dome-shaped wigwams were covered with bark or rushes, depending on the area and the preference of the Indians. They were considered to be experts in the use of the birch bark canoe and depended upon hunting, fishing, and trapping for their livelihood.

The Chippewa were divided into several bands, and were distinguished from each other by the number of blue or black lines tattooed on their cheeks and foreheads.

They were generally robust, their complexions dark, their features broad, and their hair straight and jet black, which seems to be the case in most of the other Indian tribes. Henry Schoolcraft, (1793-1864), famous Indian agent for the U.S. government, an expert on Indian affairs and ethnology, says that about one-half of the men in the Chippewa tribe in 1822, were six feet tall or over.

The appearance of the women was more agreeable than

CHIPPEWA CANOE

W. KUBIAK

CHIPPEWA DANDY

that of the men; they wore their hair very long and paid much attention to arranging it, oiling it with bear's grease, and braiding it with considerable taste.

The Chippewa seemed to be more particularly concerned with the comforts of their dress and less worried about its appearance than some of the other Indian tribes. Deer skins, dressed with the hair still on, composed their shirt or coat, which was usually encircled round the waist with a belt or sash, and hung halfway down the thigh. Their moccasins and leggins were sometimes sewn together, the latter meeting the belt to which they were fastened. A collar or scarf-like garment circled the neck, and the skin of a deer's head was formed into an unusual type of hood-like cap. They also wore turbans made of fur and in later years of

CHIPPEWA MOCCASIN

woven sash. A robe made of several deer skins sewn together was wrapped over the body; this dress was worn single for summer wear, but in winter it was always made double, the furry side forming both the lining and the outside.

The Chippewa believed that a mysterious power, similar to a spirit, resides in all animate and inanimate objects. These objects, called *Manitus,* were said to be very active in the summer, but in a dormant stage during the winter after the first snow fell.

There were approximately twenty-five thousand Chippewa in 1764. In 1783 and again in 1794 they were numbered to be roughly fifteen thousand, in 1843 about thirty thousand, and in 1851 about twenty-eight thousand. These figures are only estimates but give some idea of the size of the Chippewa tribe in early times.

CHIPPEWA IN LIGHT WINTER DRESS

One of the oldest occupations in America, the art of trapping, was mastered and practiced to perfection by the American Indian. In fact, some of their methods were so well perfected that early European trappers in this region, after seeing how productive these methods were, adopted some of them, sometimes with innovations. The Indians, in turn, after trading with the white men, adopted their steel or iron traps. Trapping was actually the main incentive of early colonization in North America. Wars were fought and many Europeans and Indians were killed for the control of the fur trade which centered around the St. Lawrence River and the Great Lakes area.

One of the earliest written accounts of how the Indians trapped beaver has been left by Paul Le Jeune. Writing in the *Jesuit Relations* of 1634, he states: "In the Spring, the Beaver is taken in a trap baited with the wood it eats. The

CHIPPEWA QUIVER

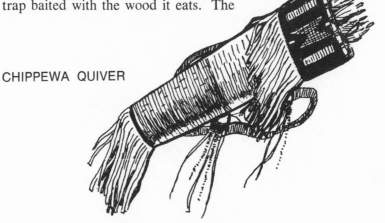

Indians understand perfectly how to handle these traps, which are made to open, when a heavy piece of wood falls upon the animal and kills it. Sometimes when the dogs encounter the Beaver outside its house, they pursue and take it easily; I have never seen this chase, but have been told of it, and the Indians highly value a dog which scents and runs down this animal.

"During the winter they capture them in nets and under the ice, in this way: They make a slit in the ice near the Beaver's house, and put into the hole a net, and some wood which serves as bait. This poor animal, searching for something to eat, gets caught in a net made of good, strong, double cord; and, emerging from the water to the opening made in the ice, they kill it with a big club."

Another account was written much later by Johann George Kohl during the years 1854-1858 in a book titled

54

Kitchi-Gami. He describes a bear trap as follows: "A piece of meat was nailed to the foot of a stout pine, as bait, and formed the attractive point de vue of a narrow, small corridor or apartment, whose walls were made of posts rammed into the ground. The entrance to this apartment is free and open, and the affair must appear peculiarly inviting to hungry Mr. Bruin. It looks as if a breakfast had been prepared for him expressly. He creeps in, for the height of the entrance is carefully calculated for his build; he needs only

to stoop a little and stretch himself. But so soon as he seizes the meat, and tries to drag it away, as if by magic a very sudden change of scenery, quite ruinous for the poor brute, takes place. Over the entrance of the hole a very long and heavy fir-tree is balanced, which is rendered still heavier by laying cross-beams and lumps of stone upon it.

CHIPPEWA CRADLEBOARD

The Canadians call it 'l'assommeur' [the bludgeon]. It lies apparently perfectly firm over the entrance, and no bear-sense could detect any connexion with the piece of meat. Still, this is produced by pieces of string in so artistic a way, that the bear need only pull the meat about a little with its paw or muzzle to bring the tremendous assommeur plump on its back. The thoughtful bear-trappers arrange the size of the cage so cleverly to the structure of the bear, that his spine is just under the assommeur when paw and snout are pushed out towards the meat. The irresistible pressure thus crushes the principal seat of the animal's muscular strength. It is said that the yell of the poor bear, when crushed beneath this merciless weight, is frequently heart-rending, and very like the cry of a suffering man. The brute must certainly have a foreboding of the fate that awaits it, and a species of contest must go on before the trap between its timidity and its hungry passion, for it will only go into the main hole when there is no other possible chance of reaching the meat. A quantity of branches and thorns are, consequently, laid over the whole apparatus, that the bear cannot possibly reach through, and only the deceitful entrance is left free. All the parts of these Canadian bear-traps have also Indian names, and hence, I believe, that it is an Indian invention adopted by the Europeans."

The most common Indian traps were the deadfall, snare, and the box trap (or hollow log trap).

DEADFALL

One of the many types of traps that may have been used by the Indians was the deadfall, which was used for capturing a variety of animals such as the beaver, otter, and bear. The mechanics of this ingenious trap were actually very simple. The trigger stick rested three to five inches above the bed log, depending on the type of prey desired. When it was pressed down ever so slightly by the unwary victim, it allowed the bent branch that held the fall log to be instantly released, bringing a crushing and almost always sure death to the unlucky victim that wandered through its deadly portal. Although the deadfall took a considerable length of time to construct, it almost always brought results.

SNARE TRAP

The spring snare or choking snare is another interesting and very effective type of trap, of which there are several varieties. In the illustration above one can see a slip-noose attached to a bent sapling or pole. In this type the trigger stick is held in the notch by the pull of the string and the moving of the bait-stick frees it from the notch. The snare or loop is commonly supported upon a series of small forked sticks so that it rests in front of the bait, just beneath the spot where the animal's head comes. The bait can be either alive or dead, depending on the individual trapper. Live bait could be a well-bound frog or any other tiny animal which would be securely bound to the bait-stick.

BOX TRAP

A very common device for trapping rabbits, opposums, and other small animals was a box trap made of a hollow log. The back was closed with a piece of board or big rock, or sometimes a stake to hold it securely in place. The front opening had a drop or sliding door, as shown in the illustration, and a trigger mechanism. This trap was the forerunner of the common box trap of today.

FOX

ALGONQUIAN STOCK

KEY

1. Theoretical location of the Fox in Michigan.
2. Early location, according to Fox legend.
3. 1670 location on Wolf River.
4. 1740 location at Little Butte des Morts.
5. Wisconsin River location.

SYNONYMOUS NAMES USED IN REFERENCE TO THE FOX

Cutagamies	Odagami	Reynards
Mechecaukis	Otagamies	Skenchiohronon
Meshkwakihug	Ouagoussac	Skuakisargi
Messenacks	Quackis	Tochewahcoo
Miskwakeeywk	Red Fox	Utagamig
Muskquaki	Renards	Wagushag
Muskwake		

FOX

The name *Fox,* is actually an English nickname for this tribe of Indians. The Fox called themselves *Meshkwakihug,* meaning "red earth people," believing they were created from red earth. Other Algonquian tribes called them *Utugamig,* which means "people of the other shore." The Sauk spoke more slowly and more clearly than the Fox did, but their languages were very similar and probably had the same origin. Possibly the two different tribes had united into one. The Fox in ancient times were very numerous and their warriors were considered to be the finest.

They were first found by the Europeans in Wisconsin, near Lake Winnebago and the Fox River area. Father Allouez had visited them as early as 1670 on the Wolf River,

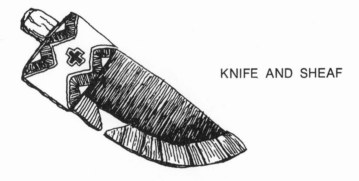

KNIFE AND SHEAF

just west of the Fox. It is believed by some that the Fox emigrated from an area in Michigan a short time prior to the Sauk migration to Wisconsin. The two tribes seem to be closely related but they do have separate identities. Fox legend relates that at one time they lived along the southern shore of Lake Superior and were forced out of this country by the Chippewa.

The French called them *Renard.* The Fox dislike for the French stemmed from the fact that the French aided the Chippewa and other tribes by trading them guns and ammunition, then gathered these tribes to try to exterminate the Fox.

Pierre Francois Xavier Charlevoix (1682-1761), a Jesuit missionary, describes the Fox: ". . . infested with their robberies and filled with murders not only the neighborhood of the Bay, their natural territory, but almost all the routes communicating with the remote colonial posts, as well as those leading from Canada to Louisiana. Except the Sioux, who often joined them, and the Iroquois, with whom they had formed an alliance."

In 1712 the Fox planned an attack on the fort at Detroit which was manned by a French garrison. The arrival of reinforcements and friendly Indians saved the fort from destruction.

The Fox continually waged war with the Illinois tribes (the Cahokia, Kaskaskia, Michigamea, Moingwena, Peoria, and Tamaroa) to the south of them, and with the help of the Sauk drove them from a large section of their domain, which the Fox took as their possession. They also waged war against the Chippewa, who lived north of them, and joined the Sioux in campaigns against them, but with little success.

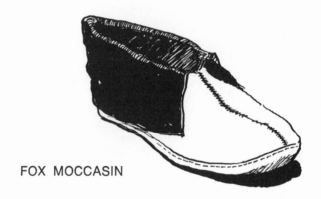

FOX MOCCASIN

The Fox lived at the Little Butte des Morts on the west bank of the Fox River during the 1740's. While occupying this area they collected tolls from travelers. Whenever a trader's canoe approached, they would place a torch on the bank of the river as a signal for them to stop and pay their tribute. They were truly professional extortionists and for this they were punished by a trader named Morand. Irate about paying tribute, he gathered a force of French and Indians to inflict punishment on the Fox. After two engagements, the Fox fled down the Wisconsin River, settling on the north bank about twenty miles from where it joins the Mississippi.

During the Revolution the Fox joined the British under De Langlade.

The Fox were almost completely wiped out in 1780 when

FOX WARRIOR

they joined the Sioux to attack the Chippewa who inhabited the area around the falls on the St. Croix River. The surviving Fox joined the Sauk.

The Fox made a treaty in 1804 and ceded lands. They joined the British in attacking Sandusky in the War of 1812 In 1824 and again in 1830, they ceded large tracts of land.

George Catlin, during his travels (1832-1839) makes some interesting comments about the Fox. He says, "The Sacs and Foxes, who were once two separate tribes, but with a language very similar, have, at some period not very remote, united into one, and are now an inseparable people, and go by the familiar appelation of the amalgam name of 'Sacs and Foxes.' " He further states, "These people . . . shave and ornament their heads, like the Osages and Pawnees, . . . and are amongst the number of tribes who have relinquished their immense tracts of lands, and recently re-

66

TOP VIEW OF A ROACH HEADPIECE

67

RED EARTH BRAVE

W. KUBIAK

tired West of the Mississippi River. Their numbers at present are not more than five or six thousand, yet they are a warlike and powerful tribe."

Their lodges contained from five to ten families each and the chiefs in the tribe were usually polygamists with as many as eight wives. In times before 1700, they carried shields made of buffalo hide.

Henry Schoolcraft mentions that he saw a band of warriors that wore headdresses made with red-dyed horsehair tied in such a way to the scalplock that it resembled a Roman helmet. The remaining part of the head was shaved and decorated with colored pigment. They also painted the upper part of their bodies and on the back of the shoulder they would place the print of a hand, probably made with white clay. Breech cloth, leggins, and moccasins were the standard dress of the times.

PEACE PIPE

ILLINOIS

ALGONQUIAN STOCK

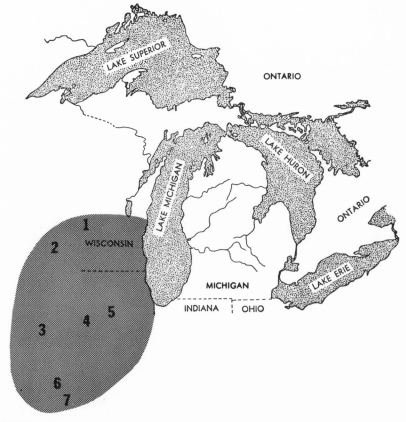

KEY

Shaded area indicates approximate territory formerly occupied by the Illinois.

1. Approximate location of 60 villages in 1660.
2. Villages on west bank of the Mississippi River in Iowa.
3. 1673 location near the mouth of the Des Moines River in Iowa.
4. 1673, two months later at Peoria.
5. 1673, a Kaskaskia village in LaSalle County.
6. 1700 location of the Kaskaskia village in Randolph County.
7. Cahokia and Tamaroa location.

SYNONYMOUS NAMES USED IN REFERENCE TO THE ILLINOIS

Alimouk	Illinese	Linneways
Cahokia	Illiniens	Michigamea
Chicktaghicks	Illinonecks	Moingwena
Eriniouai	Illuni	Ondataouatouat
Hiliniki	Isle Aux Noix	Peoria
Ilimouek	Kaskaskia	Tamaroa
Ilinois	Kicktages	

ILLINOIS

The Illinois were actually a confederacy of six Indian tribes — the Cahokia, Kaskaskia, Michigamea, Moingwena, Peoria, and Tamaroa. The name *Illinois* is a combination of Algonquian and French — *illini* (Algonquian) means "man," *ois* (French) means "is." Thus we have "man is" or "is man." Jacques Marquette mentions in his report in 1673 that, "When one speaks the word *Illinois* it is as if one said in their language, 'the men,' as if the other Indians were looked upon by them merely as animals. It must also be admitted that they have an air of humanity which we have not observed in the other nations that we have seen upon our route . . ."

They formerly occupied southern Wisconsin, northern Illinois, and parts of Iowa and Missouri. In 1660 they lived in approximately sixty villages, some southwest of Green Bay, Wisconsin, some on the west bank of the Mississippi River in Iowa, and the largest portion of the tribes in northern Illinois, along the Illinois River. Marquette found the Moinqwena and Peoria living on the west bank of the Mississippi River around the mouth of the Des Moines River in 1673. Two months later, on his return trip, he discovered them living on the Illinois River where the city of Peoria now stands. He then went north and visited a Kaskaskia village of seventy-four cabins which was situated on the upper Illinois River in what is now LaSalle County. The Kaskaskia in 1673 were living in close harmony with the Peoria.

Marquette made the following interesting observations while visiting the Illinois in 1673: ". . . They are divided into many villages, some of which are quite distant from that of which we speak, which is called peouarea. This causes some difference in their language, which, on the whole, resembles allgonguin, so that we easily understood each other. They are of gentle tractable disposition; we experienced this in the reception which they gave us. They have several wives, of whom they are extremely jealous; they watch them very closely, and cut off their noses or ears when they misbehave. I saw several women who bore the marks of their misconduct. Their bodies are shapely; they are active and very skillful with their bows and arrows. They also use guns, which they buy from our Indian allies who trade with our french. They use them especially to inspire, through

72

ILLINOIS CAPTAIN

W.KUBIAK

ILLINOIS, EARLY 19TH CENTURY

their noise and smoke, terror in their enemies; the latter do not use guns, and have never seen any, since they live too far toward the West. . . . When the Illinois depart to go to war, the whole village must be notified by a loud shout, which is uttered at the doors of their cabins, the night and the morning before their departure. The captains are distinguished from the warriors by wearing red scarfs. These are made, with considerable skill, from the hair of bears and wild cattle. They paint their faces with red ochre, great quantities of which are found at a distance of some days' journey from the village. . . . Their cabins are very large, and are roofed and floored with mats made of rushes. They make all their utensils of wood, and their ladles of the heads of cattle, whose skulls they know so well how to prepare that they use these ladles with ease for eating their sagamite. . . . Their garments consist only of skins; the women are always clad very modestly and very becomingly, while the men do not take the trouble to cover themselves."

In 1700 the Kaskaskia separated from the Peoria and after leaving them were prompted to stop in southern Illinois at the spot named after their tribe. The Cahokia and Tamaroa were living at this time on the Mississippi River in southern Illinois. The Sioux and Fox were their constant tormentors, so for their own protection they concentrated most of their population on the Illinois River at the time of La Salle's visit. Also about this time the Iroquois were waging war against the Illinois and their numbers were greatly diminished during the several years it continued. Pontiac, the famous Ottawa chief, was killed by an Illinois brave in 1769. This probably motivated the northwest tribes against them. This war almost completely exterminated the Illinois. The fortunate few who escaped this frightful experience took refuge with the French at Kaskaskia in Randolph County, Illinois, which had been settled by the French sometime between 1673 and 1700. By the year 1800 there were approximately 150 Illinois still surviving, and in 1833 the few remaining sold their land holdings in Illinois and were moved west of the Mississippi River. Later they were moved to the northwest corner of Oklahoma, where they are now living.

KICKAPOO

ALGONQUIAN STOCK

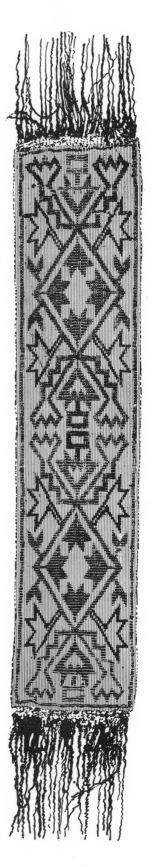

KEY

1. Early theoretical location of Kickapoo.
2. Location at portage between the Fox and Wisconsin rivers.
3. 1699 location on the Kickapoo River.
4. 1763 location in the Wabash River area.
5. 1768 location on lower end of the Illinois River.

SYNONYMOUS NAMES USED IN REFERENCE TO THE KICKAPOO

Gikapu	Kickabeux	Quincopous
Gokapatagans	Kickapoux	Shakekahquah
Ikadu	Kikapous	Shigapo
Kehabous	Qnicapous	Tekapu
Kekaupoag	Quinaquois	Yuntarayerunu

KICKAPOO

Due to their close relationship with the Sauk and Fox, who are both believed to have resided in Michigan at an early time in history, it is possible that the Kickapoo also were early residents of Michigan.

The name *Kickapoo* means "he stands about" or "he moves about, standing now here, now there."

The Kickapoo were first discovered by the French in the last half of the seventeenth century, near the portage between the Fox and Wisconsin rivers. They were great rovers and were closely allied with the Miami tribe.

In 1699 Pierre Le Sueur (1657-1705), a French trader, mentions that in his travels up the Mississippi River he discovered the river of the Quincopous, located above the

KICKAPOO PRAYER STICK

mouth of the Wisconsin River, "which," he says, "is so called from the name of a nation which formerly dwelt on its banks." It is believed that this river is the Kickapoo River in Crawford County, Wisconsin.

A few years later some of this tribe moved southeast and settled on the Milwaukee River. In 1712 they joined the Fox in an attack upon the fort at Detroit. In 1747 they were reduced to approximately eighty warriors.

They joined Pontiac in his conspiracy in 1763 but later made peace with the British.

When the Illinois confederacy was destroyed in about 1765 by combined northern tribes, the conquered country was divided by the three victors — the Sauk and Fox moving to the Rock River area and the Kickapoo moving farther south. About 1768, after the close of the war with the Illinois, the Kickapoo took possession of a Peoria village and formed their principal site at this place. Father Marquette,

78

KICKAPOO BRAVE

W.KUBIAK

KICKAPOO CHIEFTAIN

on his return trip from the South found that the Peoria Indians had moved near the lower end of the Illinois River. It seems the Kickapoo gradually extended their area. Some of the tribe settled on the Sangamon River while the rest established themselves on the Wabash River.

Being hostile towards the Americans, they gradually left their settlement on the Wabash and by 1791 it was completely abandoned. It was not until 1795 at the Treaty of Greenville that they were entirely subdued, following Anthony Wayne's decisive victory. They then ceded part of their land holdings for a small annuity. In 1799 they joined George Rogers Clark on his expedition against the British in the Northwest. In the early part of the nineteenth century they made more concessions — the lands on the Wabash and Vermilion rivers (1809) and the central portion of Illinois (1819). During the War of 1812 they aided Tecumseh in his fight against the United States. Many Kickapoo fought with Black Hawk in 1832. About one hundred Kickapoo warriors were among the Indians that the United States engaged in 1837 to fight the Seminoles in Florida. In 1854 some of the tribe settled in Kansas but, becoming dissatisfied, some of them moved to Mexico.

While living on the east side of the Mississippi River, the Kickapoo often traveled across the plains and prairies to hunt the great bison. They were introduced to the horse early in their history while on these hunting trips. They would travel as far as Texas to steal horses and mules from the Comanche nation, whose warriors were noted for their horsemanship. The Kickapoo were well acquainted with the various Indian tribes of the Plains, but even with this close contact, they retained essentially the cultural habits of the Sauk and Fox tribes.

The Kickapoo population in 1759 is estimated to have been approximately three thousand and in 1825 approximately twenty-two hundred. Their population continued to decrease quite rapidly during the nineteenth century.

MARAMEG

ALGONQUIAN STOCK

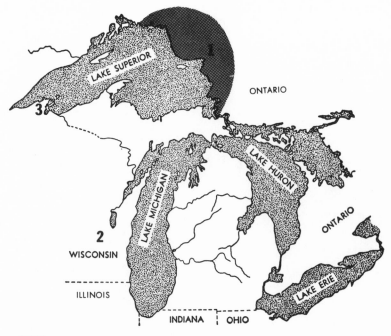

KEY

1. Earliest known location (about 1670).
2. Location on the Fox River, 1672-1673.
3. Possible location at Bayfield in 1697.

SYNONYMOUS NAMES USED IN REFERENCE TO THE MARAMEG

Gens de la Barbue   Malamechs   Malanas

MARAMEG

Very little legend or history prevails about this obscure Indian tribe. The name *Marameg*, a Chippewa word, means "catfish." This tribe, believed to be very closely related to the Chippewa, was first mentioned by Claude Dablon, a Jesuit missionary, in 1670, when they were living around the eastern half of the northern shore of Lake Superior. At this time they were living in close harmony with the Chippewa of Sault Ste. Marie. Fish were plentiful in this area, guaranteeing both tribes a sufficient food supply.

At an early date in history, the Marameg seem to have been absorbed by the Chippewa and thus lost their own tribal identity. The *Jesuit Relations* of 1672-1673 mentions them in the close vicinity of the Mascouten, who at this

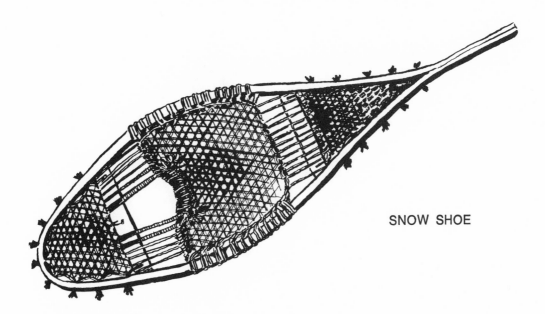

SNOW SHOE

time were residing on the banks of the Fox River in Wisconsin. It is possible that in 1697 at least some of them lived at the present site of Bayfield, Wisconsin, on the south shore of Lake Superior.

It is hopeless to try to determine the past population of this tribe since so little European contact was made with them.

They most likely resembled the Cree and Chippewa in dress, stature, and habits.

MARAMEG IN WINTER DRESS

MASCOUTENS

ALGONQUIAN STOCK

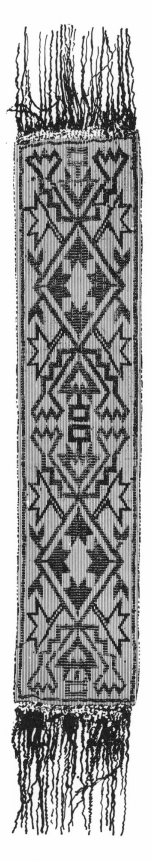

KEY

1. In 1612, Champlain believed the Mascouten lived in the area of Saginaw Bay. This is the approximate location of the Mascouten as indicated on Champlain's map of 1632.
2. Emmet County location.
3. Washtenaw or Grand River location.
4. St. Joseph location.
5. Chicago location.
6. 1670 location at the portage between the Fox and Wisconsin rivers.
7. 1680 location at Lake Winnebago.
8. 1736 location south of Green Bay, population 400. Same location in 1764, population 500.

SYNONYMOUS NAMES USED IN REFERENCE TO THE MASCOUTEN

Asistagueronon	Mascoaties	Mushkodainsug
Assistgueronons	Mascontires	Mushquatas
Attistaeronons	Mascoueteches	Musketoons
Attiste	Mascoutins	Muskuta
Fire Indians	Mashcode	Musquitans
Fire Nation	Mashkotens	Nation du Feu
Gens de Feu	Maskoutins	Nation of Fire
Little Prairie Indians	Mathkoutench	Odistastagheks
Makoutensak	Meadow Indians	

MASCOUTEN

Much mystery cloaks the Mascouten, due to the fact that there is very little written history relating to this tribe. Those who were fortunate enough to meet and live with them did not make it a point to describe them in detail, making it impossible to give a true and clear picture of them.

The Mascouten were known by the French as *Les Gens De Feu* ("The People of Fire"). The Huron called them *Assistaeronon* ("Fire People"). The Fox called them *Muskuta* and the Chippewa called them *Mashcode,* both meaning "Prairie" or "Prairie People." The Potawatomi have used the name *Mashkotens* when referring to that part of the tribe called the *Prairie Band*, which was found living on the prairies of northern Illinois.

George Catlin mentions the Mascouten during his eight years of travel among the Indian tribes of America (1832-1839). He says, "I left Rock Island about eleven o'clock in the morning, and at half-past three in a pleasant afternoon, in the cool month of October, ran my canoe to the shore of Mas-co-tin Island, where I stepped out upon its beautiful pebbly beach, with my paddle in my hand, having drawn the bow of my canoe, as usual, on to the beach, so as to hold it in its place. This beautiful island is so called from a band of the Illinois Indians of that name, who once dwelt upon it."

It is not believed that they were a distinct tribe. Henry Schoolcraft held the opinion that the Mascouten and Kickapoo were of one tribe. The Mascouten had close relationships with the Sauk, who are believed by some to have had villages at a very early time in the Saginaw Bay area of the lower peninsula of Michigan.

The first mention of the Mascouten in historical writing is made by Samuel de Champlain (1567-1635), early French explorer of the St. Lawrence River and founder of Quebec. In the year 1616, he locates them on his map as *Assistgueronons,* beyond and south of Lake Huron, the existence of Lake Michigan being unknown at the time. He mentions that the Ottawa were at war with them.

Gabriel Sagard, a Franciscan friar, says in his *Historie du Canada,* that in 1636 the Mascouten were nine or ten days' journey west of the south end of Georgian Bay. The *Jesuit Relations* of the year 1640 states that they were at war

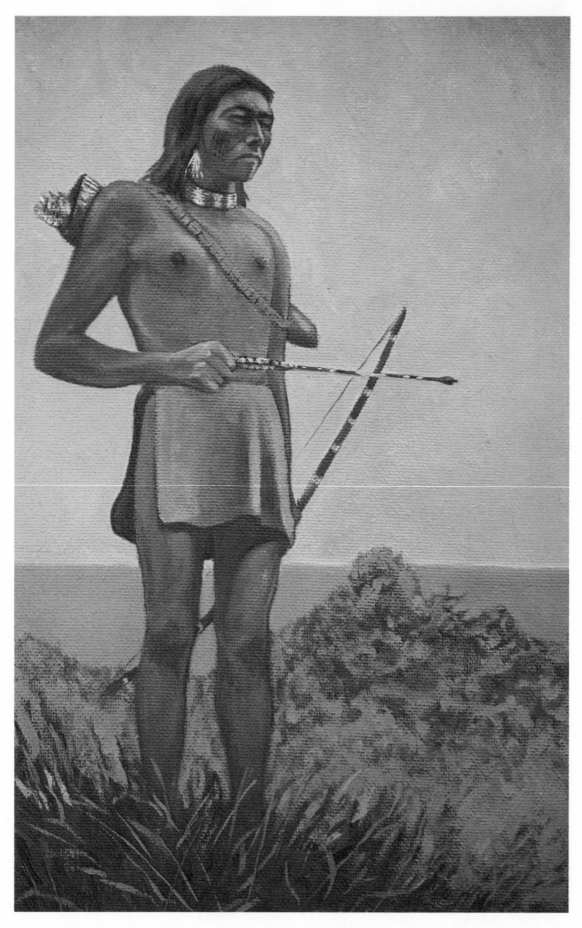

MASCOUTEN HUNTER

with the Neutrals, who were allies of the Ottawa nation. Again in 1646 the *Jesuit Relations* says that up to that date the Mascouten had never seen any Europeans. They were visited in 1673 by Jacques Marquette (1637-1675), who made a long journey by canoe by way of the Illinois River to the Mississippi and down that river to Arkansas.

Marquette has left an account of this voyage in his journal. He found the Mascouten in their village at the portage between the Fox and Wisconsin rivers, living with the Miami and Kickapoo. Marquette mentions that the Mascouten and Kickapoo were a ruder type of people than the Miami and seemed peasants by comparison. He also observed that they lived in cabins made of rushes, which didn't afford them much protection. They could be rolled up, however, and were easily transported whenever necessary.

The Mascouten are also mentioned by Louis Hennepin (164?-1701), a missionary who claimed to be the first to descend to the mouth of the Mississippi, though this claim is open to dispute. He describes the Mascouten as being very clownish and differing distinctly from the Miami. It is believed that the Mascouten, along with the Kickapoo, had a reputation for treachery and deceit, and were of an uneasy and warlike nature. The missionaries said that the Mascouten worshiped the sun and thunder, but did not practice rites nor honor a variety of minor deities as did many Indian tribes.

In 1712 the Mascouten and the Kickapoo joined the Fox as allies against the French. In this same year the Potawatomi and other northern tribes attacked the Fox and the Mascouten at the siege of Detroit, taking prisoners and killing almost two thousand Fox and Mascouten. By 1780 the Mascouten seem to have faded from history. Probably the Sauk and Fox absorbed the northern group and the Kickapoo the southern group.

Ottawa legend has it that early in the seventeenth, or possibly late in the sixteenth century, the Mascouten lived in Michigan in what is now Emmet County, their main village being in what is now the northeastern part of Friendship Township. There they cultivated large fields of corn. They were a small tribe and a peaceful people and only rarely did they send war parties to attack other tribes.

But one day a war party of Ottawa braves passed a small Mascouten village located at what is now called Seven Mile Point. They had lost some of their warriors in a raid against the Sauk and were wailing for the dead in the traditional Indian manner. As they tried to beach their canoes, the young men of the Mascouten village threw balls of ashes wrapped in green leaves at them, to show their displeasure at the Ottawa attack on their neighbors.

The Ottawa, being a small group, were forced to retreat, but upon arriving in their own villages they told of this humiliating experience. Being a proud people, the Ottawa felt this disgraceful insult could only be avenged by the blood of the Mascouten and they joined forces with the Chippewa to exterminate them.

An old man in the main Mascouten village warned his people that they would soon be attacked by the Ottawa and recommended that they seek safety in some other area. But no one heeded the warning, so he with his sons and their families moved to the shore of Little Traverse Bay, where Harbor Springs is now located. The predicted battle ensued, the fiercest battle ever fought in this area, and only one survivor, a young Mascouten, escaped to inform the people at Little Traverse Bay about the massacre.

It was probably during this time that the Mascouten and Assegun became confederates (see *Assegun*).

The residents in some of the outlying villages of the Mascouten escaped the fate of their relatives and they moved south where they established themselves near the St. Joseph River. The old cleared fields and garden beds of this area are attributed to these people.

Later the Ottawa traded with the French for firearms and determined to complete the annihilation of their old enemies, the Mascouten. A war party, eager to try the newly acquired weapons on the unsuspecting foe, set out for the St. Joseph River settlement. The Mascouten, having never before seen guns or gunpowder, mistook the firearms carried by their attackers for war clubs and came out to meet them with bows and arrows. The result was utter chaos, and the remnants of the tribe were scattered, some to the Chicago area. Later they sought safety to the south and west.

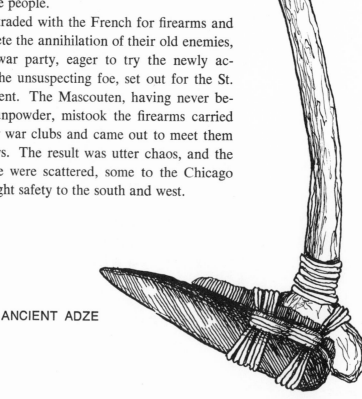

ANCIENT ADZE

MASCOUTEN IN SUMMER DRESS

MENOMINEE

ALGONQUIAN STOCK

KEY

1. Early location of the Menominee and Noquet.
2. Bay de Noc location.
3. 1634 Menominee River location.
   Shaded area indicates the general region of Menominee habitation.

SYNONYMOUS NAMES USED IN REFERENCE TO THE MENOMINEE

Addle Heads	Malouminek	Nation of Wild Oats
Des Nocques	Manomines	Omanomini
Folles Avoines	Melomelinoia	Rice Indians
Les Folles	Menomenes	Wild Oat Indians
Mahnomoneeg	Menomoni	Wild Rice Eaters
Malhomines	Monomonees	Wild Rice Men
Malhominy	Moon Calves	Wild Rice People
Malomimis	Nation de la folle avoine	

MENOMINEE

The Menominee Indians are known as the *"Wild Rice People,"* as their name implies in the Chippewa tongue. In *The Indian Tribes of North America,* McKenny and Hall state, "The Menominees, or Folles Avoines, inhabit the country between the lakes and the Mississippi River, their principal residence being west of Lake Michigan, whence they stray into the country of the Winnebagoes, who are their friends. Their language is peculiar, and difficult to be learned by white men. . . . The early writers all speak of them in favourable terms, not only as 'very fine men, the best shaped of all Canada,' but as possessing an agreeable personal appearance, indicative of more neatness, and of a greater taste for ornament than that of any other of our north-western Indians. But they are now greatly degener-

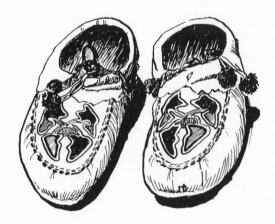

MENOMINEE MOCCASINS

ated, . . . in consequence of their intercourse with the whites, and their fatal propensity for ardent spirits."

McKenny and Hall continue: "They are of a lighter complexion than the Indians around them, from whom also they differ in being less fierce and warlike. Though brave, they are peaceable, subsisting chiefly on the wild rice or false oats, . . . and avoiding, either from indolence or a dislike of war, the quarrels in which their neighbors are continually engaged. The women are patient, obedient, and laborious, and when introduced into the families of the traders residing in the wilderness, are preferred as domestics to those of the other Indian Tribes. We know little of the history of this people."

MENOMINEE, 19TH CENTURY

Some of the earliest known locations of the Menominee were at Bay de Noc in the upper peninsula of Michigan and the Menominee River between Wisconsin and Michigan. Those living at Bay de Noc at the mouth of Green Bay were called by the French, *Des Noques,* which may be interpreted as *Noquet. No'ke* means "bear foot" in the Chippewa language. These people also were of Algonquian stock, and according to the French their territory extended from Bay de Noc across the upper peninsula of Michigan to Lake Superior.

In all probability Jean Nicolet, a trader, was the first Frenchman to encounter the Menominee. He visited them in 1634 at the mouth of the Menominee River. At times their villages extended to the Fox River and in their Treaty of 1831 with the United States, they claimed possession of the land from the mouth of Green Bay to the mouth of the Milwaukee River and west from Green Bay to Lake Supe-

MENOMINEE CANOE

W. KUBIAK

MENOMINEE WITH TYPICAL HEAD DRESS

MENOMINEE AND ACCOMPANIST

rior, including the headwaters of the Fox and Menominee rivers. They continued to live in this area until 1852.

According to the *Jesuit Relations* of 1671, the Menominee were driven from the lands lying just south of Michilimackinac, where some of the Noquet lived when first discovered by the French. It is likely that the Menominee and the Noquet comprised two branches of one tribe. Later the Noquet tribe disappeared completely from all historical accounts, probably being absorbed by the Menominee or Chippewa.

The Menominee claimed to understand the Sauk, Fox, and Kickapoo dialects but found the Chippewa, Ottawa, and Potawatomi dialects unfamiliar. This probably proves a closer kinship to the first three.

100

MENOMINEE BOW

Charlevoix mentions in his journal, written in 1721, that "After we had advanced five or six leagues, we found ourselves abreast of a little island, which lies near the western side of the bay, and which concealed from our view, the mouth of a river, on which stands the village of the Malhomines Indians, called by our French Folles Avoines or Wild Oat Indians, probably from their living chiefly on this sort of grain. The whole nation consists only of this village, and that too not very numerous. 'Tis really a great pity, they being the finest and handsomest men in all Canada. They are even of a larger stature than the Poutewatamies. I have been assured that they had the same original and nearly the same language with the Noquets and the Indians at the falls [Sault St. Marie]. But they add that they have likewise a language peculiar to themselves, which they never

W. KUBIAK

MENOMINEE WOMAN WITH TUMPLINE

communicate. I have also been told several stories of them, as of a serpent which visits their village every year, and is received with much ceremony, which makes me believe them a little addicted to witchcraft."

Zebulon M. Pike (1779-1813), who explored the Mississippi to its source in 1805, describes the men of this tribe as "straight and well made, about the middle size; their complexions generally fair for Indians, their teeth good, their eyes large and rather languishing; they have a mild but independent expression of countenance that charms at first sight."

Their beliefs and rituals were practically the same as the Chippewa's. During the nineteenth century their population varied from about twelve hundred to twenty-five hundred.

The Menominee were allied with the French and marched to the aid of Detroit in 1712. Later they drove the Fox from Green Bay, Wisconsin. During the Revolutionary War and also the War of 1812 they became allies of the British. The Menominee assisted in the capture of Mackinac in 1812, and aided Tecumseh (176?-1813), a chief of the Shawnee, at Fort Meigs and Fort Stephenson in 1813. Subsequently they made several treaties with the United States, also aiding the Americans against the Sauk and Fox during the Black Hawk War of 1832.

MENOMINEE QUIVER

MIAMI

ALGONQUIAN STOCK

KEY

Shaded area indicates main area of Miami habitation.

1. First recorded location, 1658.
2. Mississippi Valley location, 1667.
3. Fox River headwaters location, 1670.
4. Chicago village location.
5. St. Joseph River village location.
6. Kalamazoo River village location.
7. Detroit village location, 1703.
8. Miami River location, about 1720 to 1763.
9. Possible Scioto River location.
10. Retirement to Indiana, 1764.

SYNONYMOUS NAMES USED IN REFERENCE TO THE MIAMI

Maiama	Omameeg	Titwa
Maumee	Omaumeg	Tuihtuihronoons
Meames	Oumami	Twechtweys
Memilounique	Oumamik	Twightwees
Metousceprinioueks	Piankashaw	Twigtwig
Myamicks	Qwikties	Twitchwees
Naked Indians	Tawatawas	Wea
Nation de la Grue		

MIAMI

The western portion of Michigan was probably occupied by the Miami at an early time in history, although they later left this area for reasons unknown. The Jesuits arrived at the St. Joseph River in 1673, naming it "River of the Miamis," because it ran through the country of these Indians. Although the Miami still inhabited the area, it is believed they were not very numerous.

The major village of the Miami was on the Kankakee River, which rises in northern Indiana and flows westward through northern Illinois. This village was visited by Sieur de La Salle, famous French explorer (1643-1687), while he tried to make peace with the Indians of the area. La

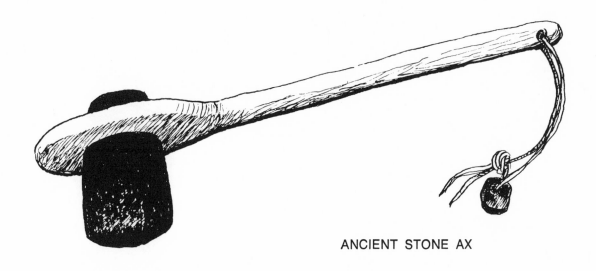

ANCIENT STONE AX

Salle accomplished his goal, but the peace was shortlived, for the Miami feared the approach of Iroquois war parties. In 1680 a party of Iroquois was returning from a foray with one of the Illinois tribes, and while traveling back toward their country they surprised a small band of Miami and killed them. They then built crude forts with brush and trees right in the center of the Miami country. The Miami appealed to La Salle to help them rid their country of the Iroquois. Responding to their pleas, he met a band of Iroquois warriors and so completely bewildered them

W.KUBIAK

MIAMI BOWMAN

by his threats that they waited for dark to steal away in the safety of the night. After this unusual victory by La Salle, the Miami gave their allegiance to the French. They also agreed to make peace with the Illinois and in 1681 removed themselves to an area near Lake Peoria. There is no doubt that their fear of the Iroquois played a major part in this relocation. After ten years had passed, a portion of the tribe returned to the St. Joseph River country. When La Salle started on his long trip to the Gulf of Mexico, eighteen warriors and ten Indian women accompanied him. The remaining Indians in the village of the Miami in the St. Joseph country soon after left for the Illinois River Valley. They did not linger there, for it was not long afterward that they were attacked by a large war party of Sioux Indians from the Northwest country. Cadillac mentions that three thousand of the Miami were killed in this tremendous massacre of 1695. The remnants of this tribe fled to Mackinac Island under the protection of the French. Here they remained until about 1706, when all Miami left Michigan and the St. Joseph country.

The French first recorded the existence of Miami at or near the mouth of Green Bay, Wisconsin, in 1658. They were referred to as *Oumamik* by the French, which possibly could be *Omaumeg* in the Chippewa language, meaning "people who live on the peninsula." Later the French called them *Maumee,* which is the French pronunciation for *Miami.* The English and the Iroquoian Confederacy called them *Twightwees.* Later they moved westward settling approximately 120 miles from Green Bay. The first actual contact with the Miami was about 1668 when Nicolas Perrot, a French fur trader, visited them. He revisited them again in 1670, when they were living with the Mascouten on the headwaters of the Fox River in a palisaded village. A short time later the Miami left the Mascouten to settle near the lower end of Lake Michigan at Chicago and on the St. Joseph River and Kalamazoo River in what is now the state of Michigan. The main Miami settlement on the St. Joseph River was about forty-five miles inland from Lake Michigan. A few years later the extent of the territory inhabited by this tribe makes one believe that the Miami in Wisconsin, whose existence was first discovered by the French, actually formed only a portion of the tribe. The remainder of the Miami were in northeastern Illinois and northern Indiana. Later the Miami were located on the

MIAMI BRAVE

Wabash River in Indiana and northwestern Ohio, where three rivers were named after them. Little Turtle (1752-1812), a celebrated chief of the Miami, relates, "My fathers kindled the first Fire at Detroit; thence they extended their lines to the headwaters of the Scioto; thence to the mouth of the Wabash, and thence to Chicago over Lake Michigan." In 1703 there was a Miami village at Detroit, although their major settlement was still on the St. Joseph River. With the intrusion of northern tribes, the Miami retreated from the St. Joseph River and the area northwest of the Wabash River to form villages on the Miami River in Ohio, and probably to the area of the Scioto River. They lived in this area until 1763, when they moved to Indiana. They participated in all the Indian wars of the Ohio Valley, up to the end of the War of 1812. By 1827 they disposed of almost all their land in Indiana and most of them moved to Kansas. There were still three hundred Miami living on a reservation in Wabash County, Indiana, in 1872.

Charlevoix believed that in earlier times the Miami and the Illinois were of the same tribe, because of the similarity of their languages, customs and ways of living. Both the Miami and Illinois cultivated their lands and lived in permanent settlements, never migrating until forced to move by neighboring warlike tribes. They were inclined to be peace loving Indians who would only defend themselves if the occasion called for it. However, Father Louis Hennepin describes them as follows, "This Village, as I have intimated, consists of three several nations, viz. Miamis, Maskoutens, and Kikabeaux. The first are more civil than the other and better shap'd, as well as more liberal. They wear long Hair over their Ears, which looks well enough. They are accounted valiant Men amongst their Neighbors; but are so cunning, that they seldom return from their warlike Expeditions without Booty. They are apt to learn any thing, for they love to hear the European's talk; and Father Allouez told me, that they had such a violent desire to be instructed, that they often disturb'd his rest to ask him questions about what he had told them the day before."

He also mentions, that "they go stark naked in Summertime, wearing only the kind of Shooes made of the Skins of Bulls; but the Winter being pretty severe in their Country, tho' very short, they wear Gowns made of the Skins of Wild Beasts, or of Bulls, which they dress and paint most curiously as I have already observ'd."

W. KUBIAK

MIAMI, 19TH CENTURY

The men were of medium height, well built, heads rather round, composure agreeable, and swift runners. The women wore deerskins, while the men were usually tattooed from head to foot. The lodges they lived in were covered with rush mats. They did most of their traveling by land rather than canoe. The Miami worshiped the sun and thunder, both of which played an important part in their lives, for they realized that sun and rain were needed to make their crops grow.

The Miami population in 1764 was estimated to be

MIAMI IN COLD WEATHER DRESS

W. KUBIAK '61

MIAMI CALLING ON HIS SECRET SPIRIT

about 1,850, and in 1765 about 1,250. These estimates are not considered accurate because of the intermingling of the Wea and Piankashaw with the Miami. In 1822 they numbered approximately 2,500, and in 1885 only 57 Miami were reported to be living in Indian territory.

The Piankashaw and Wea are considered subtribes of the Miami, although they probably were all one tribe in early years, achieving separate identity in later years. The Wea and Piankashaw spoke languages that are almost identical to that of the Miami and they possessed the same traits, factors which lend credence to the supposition that at one time they were one tribe. Antoine de la Mothe Cadillac (1658-1730), French founder of Detroit, said that the Piankashaw and Wea lived west of the Miami village on the St. Joseph River in Michigan, living with the Mascouten, Kickapoo, and other tribes. It is possible that they were located on the Vermilion River in Indiana and Illinois. In later history the Piankashaw and Wea joined with the Peoria and Kaskaskia, who were also known as the Illinois. The Wea moved from the area of Illinois and Indiana under the treaty of 1820; the Piankashaw also migrated from this same country voluntarily.

113

CATLINITE PIPE STEM

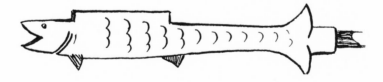

MISSISAUGA

ALGONQUIAN STOCK

KEY

1. First encountered by the French (1634) on the Mississagi River and Manitoulin Island.
2. Manitoulin Island location.
3. Eighteenth century location.
4. A small settlement in 1708.
5. 1746 location near Detroit(?).
6. 1750 location near the Seneca River.

SYNONYMOUS NAMES USED IN REFERENCE TO THE MISSISAUGA

Achsissaghecs	Messissauga	Mississaugies
Aoechisacronon	Michesaking	Mussisakies
Awechisaehronon	Missaugees	Nation de Bois
Ishisagek Roanu	Missiagos	Oumisagai
Massasaugas	Missisak	Poils leue
Messagnes	Mississaguras	Sissisaguez

MISSISAUGA

The name *Missisauga* means, in the Chippewa language, "large outlet," probably referring to the mouth of the Missisagi River. The Missisauga tribe is closely related to the Chippewa. At one time it was thought that they actually were a part of the Chippewa tribe, but now it is generally accepted that they were a distinct tribe.

The Missisauga lived near the mouth of the river which bears their tribal name, on the north shore of Lake Huron

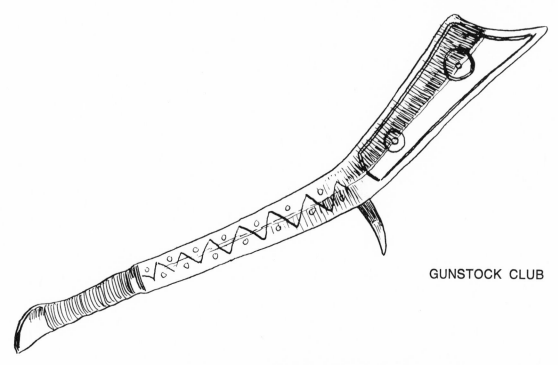

GUNSTOCK CLUB

and also on bordering Manitoulin Island. They were first discovered by the French in 1634.

Having a strong desire to trade with the Europeans early in the eighteenth century, the Missisauga began to migrate in a south-eastwardly direction, to where the Huron formerly resided, in the area lying between Lake Huron, Georgian Bay, and Lake Erie. In 1720 the French opened a trading post on the west end of Lake Ontario to trade with the Missisauga. By 1736 segments of this tribe were found at various locations on the Missisagi River, Manitoulin Island, Lake St. Clair, the Toronto River, and on the west end of Lake Ontario. The French,

118

MISSISAUGA WARRIOR

W.KUBIAK

aided by the Ottawa, finally forced most of the Missisauga from this area. Some of them resettled near the Seneca (one of the five Iroquois nations) on the east side of Lake Erie; a few managed to remain in their native land.

In 1746 they became the seventh tribe to join the Iroquois league of nations, at which time they were living in five villages near Detroit. It is possible that those who settled with the Seneca were first established in the vicinity of Detroit and then moved to live with the Seneca. This alliance with the Iroquois terminated at the outbreak of the French and Indian War (1754-1763).

119

BRAVE ON THE CHASE

It is impossible to estimate accurately the population of this tribe because of the confusion which results when one tries to separate them from the Chippewa and other Algonquian tribes who were closely related to them. In 1736 there were approximately 1,300, some 250 of which were on Manitoulin Island and along the Mississagi River. The rest resided on the Ontario Peninsula. In 1778 it was estimated that there were close to 1,250 on the north side of Lake Erie, but by 1884 their number had dwindled to 744.

NIPISSING

ALGONQUIAN STOCK

KEY

1. First known location on Lake Nipissing in 1613.
2. About 1650-1667 on Lake Nipigon.
3. Back to original location in 1671.
4. Three Rivers (Trois-Rivières) location.
5. The Oka location.

SYNONYMOUS NAMES USED IN REFERENCE TO THE NIPISSING

Askikouaneronons
Bisserains
Ebicerinys
Longs Cheveux
Nation des Sorciers
Nebicerine

Nepicerinis
Nepisinguis
Nibissiriniens
Nipissirinioek
Odishk-wa-gami

O-dish-quag-um-eeg
Quiennontateronons
Skecaneronons
Sorcerers
Tiskwawgomeeg

NIPISSING

The name *Nipissing* means "little-water people." They were first discovered by the French in 1613 on the shores of the lake in Ontario, Canada, bearing their name. They have been residing there off and on ever since they were first encountered. In 1650 they were attacked by the Iroquois, who killed many of their tribe. The fortunate few who survived retreated to Lake Nipigon, where later Claude Jean Allouez (1622-1689) met them in 1667. In a short time, about 1671, they moved back to Lake Nipissing, their original homeland. Some of the tribe later moved to Three Rivers (Trois Rivières) on the St. Lawrence River, while others stayed with the Iroquois at Oka, which is situated on Lake of Two Mountains, an expansion of the Ottawa

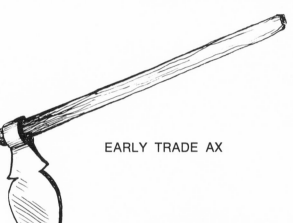

EARLY TRADE AX

River about thirty-six miles from Montreal. They seemed to be a peace loving people and very staunch friends of the French. They lived in permanent villages, but upon occasion during the fall months, would travel south to the Huron settlements to fish and prepare food for the coming of winter. They did not raise crops to any extent, because the land in the area does not lend itself to cultivation being covered, with only a few exceptions, by rock and dense forests of evergreens. They would barter with the Cree Indians to the north and with the Huron Indians to the south.

The Nipissing were so beset with spirits and infested with demons and magicians that the French dubbed them *The Sorcerers.* In 1884 the Nipissing were said to have numbered 162.

NIPISSING SORCERER

OTTAWA

ALGONQUIAN STOCK

KEY

Black area indicates legendary habitat of the Ottawa Indians.

1. Meeting place of Champlain and the Cheveux Releves, 1615.
2. About 1649, located on the islands at the entrance to Green Bay.
3. Keweenaw Bay location of 1660.
4. Island location near the entrance to Lake Pepin.
5. Chequamegon Bay location.
6. 1680 St. Ignace location.
7. Settlements about 1700.
8. L'Arbre Croche settlement about 1708.

Shaded areas indicate various locations of the Ottawa after the above dates.

SYNONYMOUS NAMES USED IN REFERENCE TO THE OTTAWA

Andatahouats	Ondataouaouat	Outaouaks
Atowas	Ontaonatz	Outauas
Attawawas	Ottahway	Outawais
Cheueux Releues	Ottaouais	Outaway
Cheveux Releves	Ottawacs	Outtaouacts
Cheveux Relevez	Ottawasse	Tawas
Keinouche	Ottawwawwug	Traders
Kiskakon	Outaoue of the Sable	Ukuayata
Nassawaketon	Outaouae Sinago	Waganhaes
Oadauwaus	Outaouaies	Watawawininiwok

OTTAWA

The name *Ottawa,* which comes from *adawa,* an Algonquian term meaning "to trade," was bestowed upon this tribe because they were great intertribal traders. They dealt mainly in furs, skins, corn, mats, sunflower oil, tobacco, and roots and herbs of medicinal value. They would trade for just about anything that caught their fancy. Due to the need for much travel while carrying on their trade, they became very proficient in handling canoes.

Indian legend says that the Ottawa, Chippewa, and Potawatomi formerly comprised one tribe or people who came from an area north of the Great Lakes to Mackinac, Michigan. Here they separated, the Ottawa locating on Manitoulin Island and along the northern and southern shores of Georgian Bay. French records from early times confirm this location of the Ottawa.

In the year 1615, on the French River, west of Lake Nipissing near the shore of Georgian Bay, Samuel de Champlain encountered a group of approximately three hundred Indians whom he promptly named the *Cheveux Relevez* because of their unusual hair styles. He says, "Not one of our Courtiers takes so much pains in dressing his locks." He also mentions that the tattoos on various parts of their bodies were of many fashions and designs. Their faces were painted and their noses pierced and decorated with trinkets. They carried arms of bows and arrows, shields of bison hide, and clubs. The only thing they were missing was clothes, it being their custom in warm weather to wear none. The Indians were busy at this time gathering berries for their winter store. However, they did not live in this area, but west and southwest of Nottawasaga Bay off Georgian Bay in what is now Bruce and Grey counties in Ontario.

The following year Champlain visited the "Cheveux Relevez" (Ottawa), in their home area, which lies west of the Huron Indians. He mentions that they were very happy to see the French again and that they had waged war with the Mascouten, who lived ten days journey from them. He records that their numbers were great and that the majority of men were a combination of warrior, hunter, and fisherman. They were ruled by many chiefs in their own separate districts and communities. He also mentions that the women

128

EARLY OTTAWA BRAVE

W. KUBIAK

YOUNG OTTAWA DANDY

wore clothing and that in winter the men wore robes of fur that covered them like a mantle, but discarded them in summer.

Jean Nicolet, a French trader, visited a portion of the Ottawa tribe who were living on Manitoulin Island during the year of 1635. They were strong allies of the French and Huron and carried on trade between the western tribes and the French.

After the Iroquois routed the Huron in 1648 and 1649, they turned upon the Ottawa, who, with a small remnant of the Huron, retreated to the islands at the entrance of Green Bay, where the Potawatomi had settled earlier.

Around 1650 the tribe consisted of four bands, the Kiska-kon, the Outaouae Sinago, Outaouae of the Sable, and Nassawaketon ("People of the Fork"). Possibly there was a fifth, the Keinouche. They later moved westward, some going to Keweenaw Bay. A small group fled with a band of Huron to the Mississippi River and settled on an island near the entrance to Lake Pepin. Here they unwisely attacked the Sioux and were forced to retreat northeast to Black River, Wisconsin, and then northward to settle on the shores of Chequamegon Bay. However, the Sioux continued to harass them, so they took advantage of a promise of protec-

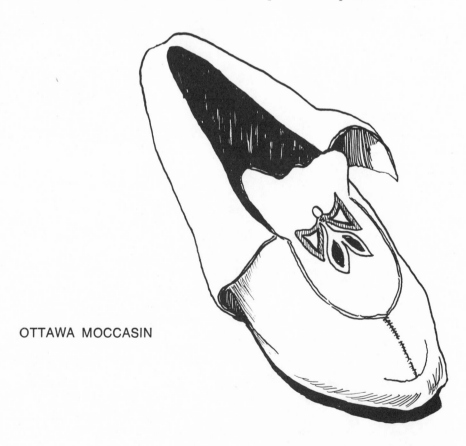

OTTAWA MOCCASIN

131

OTTAWA CHIEF

OTTAWA FINDING A MEDICINE ARROW

tion by the French and returned to Manitoulin Island in 1670 and 1671. Their stay here was brief and by 1680 most of them had joined the Huron at Mackinac around the Mission of St. Ignace, established by Marquette in 1671.

The Ottawa and Huron lived together until about 1700, when a portion of the Ottawa tribe seems to have started a small settlement on the west shore of Lake Huron between Saginaw Bay and Detroit, while the Huron moved to an area around the present city of Detroit. A small band returned from the southeastern part of the lower peninsula of Michigan, where they had moved previously, to Mackinac about 1706. Later the main portion of the tribe settled at Waganakisi (L'Arbre Croche). It was from this area that they began to spread in many directions, with the main body settling on the east shore of Lake Michigan as far south as the St. Joseph River. Some went to southern Wisconsin and northeastern Illinois; others lived on Manitoulin Island with the Chippewa; still others located on the shore of Lake Erie from Detroit through the northern part of the present state of Ohio to the area of Beaver River in Pennsylvania. They were active in the Indian wars of that region until the end of the War of 1812.

BRASS PIPE AX ABOUT 1800

OTTAWA TRADER

Pontiac, an Ottawa chief of note who was born in 1720, was one of the most successful of the Indian chiefs opposing the British. He led the combined forces of Ottawa, Chippewa, and Potowatomi. Though he consented to the surrender of Detroit to the British at the end of the French and Indian War, he later organized a widespread conspiracy in 1762, a prominent event in Ottawa history. Assembling a large force near Detroit, he fired up his warriors by his gifted oration, but his plot was disclosed and his siege of the city from May to October 1763, was fruitless. However, many other British posts — Sandusky, Michilimackinac, Presque Isle — fell before Pontiac's allies. Pontiac signed a treaty in 1766, and three years later he was murdered.

A small segment of the tribe that refused to submit to the authority of the United States moved to Canada and settled on Walpole Island in Lake St. Clair. The remaining Ottawa in Canadian territory reside on Manitoulin and Cockburn islands and along the adjacent shores of Lake Huron. A great number of Ottawa live today in a number of scattered villages and settlements in the lower peninsula of Michigan.

OTTAWA BOW

W. KUBIAK '63

FRIENDLY OFFERING
FROM AN OTTAWA VISITOR

POTAWATOMI

ALGONQUIAN STOCK

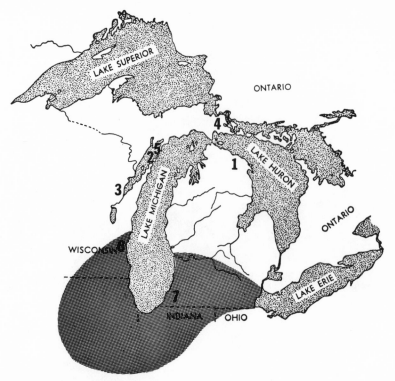

KEY

1. Possible early location of the Potawatomi (prior to 1615).
2. Approximate location when first encountered by the French.
3. Location in Winnebago area (up to 1640).
4. Location at Sault Ste. Marie, 1641.
5. Location on islands in the mouth of Green Bay, 1670.
6. Location on Milwaukee River at close of seventeenth century.
7. St. Joseph River location at close of seventeenth century.
   Shaded area indicates the approximate area held by the Potawatomi at the beginning of the nineteenth century.

SYNONYMOUS NAMES USED IN REFERENCE TO THE POTAWATOMI

Asistagueronon	Pattawatomie	Poutewatamies
Atsistarhonon	Pedadumies	Putawatame
Attistae	Poes	Putawatimies
Fire Nation	Potewatamik	Putewata
Gens de Feu	Pottawattami	Undatomatendi
Nation du Feu	Pottawattomi	Wahhonahah
Nation of Fire	Pottowotomees	Wapoos
Patawatimes	Pouteaouatami	Woraqe

POTAWATOMI

The name *Potawatomi,* which is derived from the Chippewa language, in all probability means "People of the place of fire." The Huron Indians, enemies of the Potawatomi, used a word in their own tongue, but with the same meaning, to designate this tribe.

Indian legend says that the Potawatomi, Chippewa, and Ottawa were once all members of one tribe who came down from the north and arrived at the upper region of Lake Huron at an early time and later divided into three separate

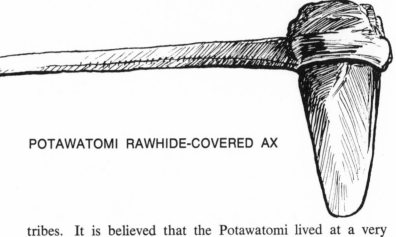

POTAWATOMI RAWHIDE-COVERED AX

tribes. It is believed that the Potawatomi lived at a very early date in the upper part of the lower peninsula of Michigan but were driven north and west by Indian adversaries into the upper peninsula of Michigan and Wisconsin. Up to the year 1640 the Potawatomi were living in the area of the Winnebago and by 1641, after retreating from the constant onslaught and harassment of the Sioux, they relocated at Sault Ste. Marie. Claude Allouez, a Jesuit missionary, in 1667 met approximately three hundred Potawatomi warriors at Chequamegon Bay. In 1670 some of the Potawatomi were reported to be living on the islands in the mouth of Green Bay. It is believed that at this time they already were moving on their southward migration. In 1679 the Potawatomi were visited by Sieur de La Salle in the Green Bay region of Wisconsin. He found them to be very friendly. At the close of the seventeenth century they situated their villages on the Milwaukee River, where Milwaukee now lies, and also on the St. Joseph River, where the Miami were established at one time. About 1765 they took posession of part of the state of Illinois, northeast of the country which had been taken over by the Sauk, Fox, and Kickapoo. They extended their territory eastward over southern Michigan and gradually spread south to the Wabash River. The Potawatomi had notified the Miami that they intended to encroach upon their land along the Wabash River, and in spite of the protests by the Miami and their claims to this region, they moved in.

At the beginning of the nineteenth century the Potawatomi resided in about fifty villages located from the Milwaukee River in Wisconsin to the Grand River in Michigan, southwestward over a great portion of northern Illinois, eastward across Michigan to Lake Erie, and southward in Indiana to the Wabash River Valley to where Pine Creek flows

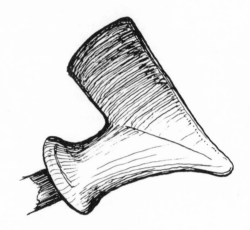

WOODEN PIPE BOWL

into the Wabash near Attica in Warren County. Thus they were in complete possession of the country surrounding the lower part of Lake Michigan.

The Potawatomi were allied with the French until the peace of 1763. They played a prominent part in Pontiac's Conspiracy, and during the opening of the Revolution in 1775, they fought against the United States until the Treaty of Greenville was signed in 1795 after the successful campaigns of General Anthony Wayne against the Northwestern tribes in the years of 1793 and 1794. This treaty called for a cessation of hostilities, required that all prisoners be returned, and that the boundary line between the Indian lands and the United States be fixed. The name of Topenibe, one of the head chiefs of the Potawatomi, appears in this treaty.

In 1810 Tecumseh, a celebrated Shawnee chief, visited the Potawatomi and enlisted their help to drive out the

POTAWATOMI BRAVE

POTAWATOMI

settlers. They failed, however, due to the superior tactics of General Harrison at Tippecanoe. This battle, which gave Harrison a grand military reputation, took place near Battle Ground, Indiana.

Some of these same Potawatomi took part in the Massacre of the River Raisin in the War of 1812, in which they sided with the English. They also cooperated with Colonel Henry Proctor of the British Army in the battle in which Tecumseh was killed in 1813. They were completely subdued in this battle. They finally signed peace treaties in 1815, but the settlers constantly encroached on them and the pressure continued.

A treaty was signed August 29, 1821, by the Ottawa,

POTAWATOMI DUGOUT

POTAWATOMI, 19TH CENTURY

Chippewa, and Potawatomi chiefs, in which they gave up their claim to all the land in Michigan south of the north bank of Grand River, but kept five reservations and certain grants of land to individual Indians. The United States in this treaty promised to pay the Potawatomi $5,000 annually for twenty years and also to appropriate $1,000 to furnish a blacksmith and a teacher for fifteen years. Later, in the treaty of September 26, 1833, at Chicago, these same three tribes ceded most of their reservation lands south of the Grand River for only $100,000.

A large number of Potawatomi in Indiana declined to leave their homeland and only in the face of superior military force were they driven out. Some of them fled to Walpole Island in Lake St. Clair. The remainder went west, settling in western Iowa and in Kansas.

In early times the Potawatomi made their clothing of tanned animal hides and furs. The men wore mocassins, leggings, breechcloths, garters, leather shirts, and sometimes belts. On their heads they wore feathers, fur turbans, and roaches. They wore fur robes and carried bandoleers over their shoulders. Clothing was decorated by painted designs and dyed quill work. Later, when trade goods were introduced, glass beads and applique work decorated their cloth-

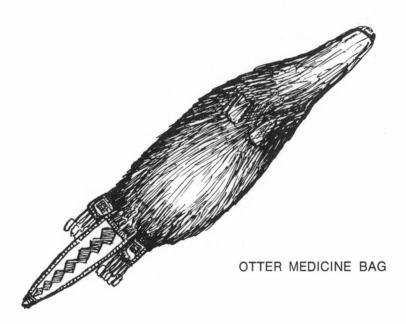

OTTER MEDICINE BAG

ing. Finger-woven sash, a muslin-like material, was worn as a turban, across the shoulders, and around the waist as a belt. They carried bags which resembled the sleeve of a woman's ruffled blouse with a drawstring at the top.

In *History of the Indian Tribes of North America,* by Thomas McKenney and James Hall, one can read the following description: ". . . Some are six foot in heighth. They have a rather dark complexion. Most of the Potawattimies whom we met with, are characterised by a low, aquiline, and well shaped nose. His eyes are small, elongated, and black; they are not set widely apart. His forehead is low and receding; the facial angle amounts to about eighty. His hair is black, and indicates a slight tendency to curl. His cheek-bones are remarkably high and prominent, even for those of an Indian; they are not, however, angular, but present very distinctly the rounded appearance which distinguishes the aboriginal American from the Asiatic." Then, describing a certain chief, they continue, "His mouth was large, the upper lip prominent. His dress was old and somewhat dirty, but appeared to have been arranged upon his person with no small degree of care. It consisted of leather leggings, buttoned on the outside, a breechcloth of blue broadcloth, and a short checkered shirt over it; the whole was covered with a blanket, which was secured round his waist by a belt, and hung not ungracefully from his shoulders, generally concealing his right arm, which is rendered useless and somewhat withered. His face was carefully painted with vermilion round his left eye. Four feathers, colored without taste, hung behind, secured to a string which was tied to a lock of his hair. In our second interview with him he wore a red and white feather in his head, that was covered with ornaments equally deficient in taste."

It was estimated that in 1658 there were 3,000 Potawatomi. Their population was reported in later years as follows: 1,500 in 1765, 2,250 in 1778, and in 1820 it is believed they numbered 3,400. Their total number never seemed to exceed this last figure.

W. KUBIAK '60

POTAWATOMI IN WINTER DRESS

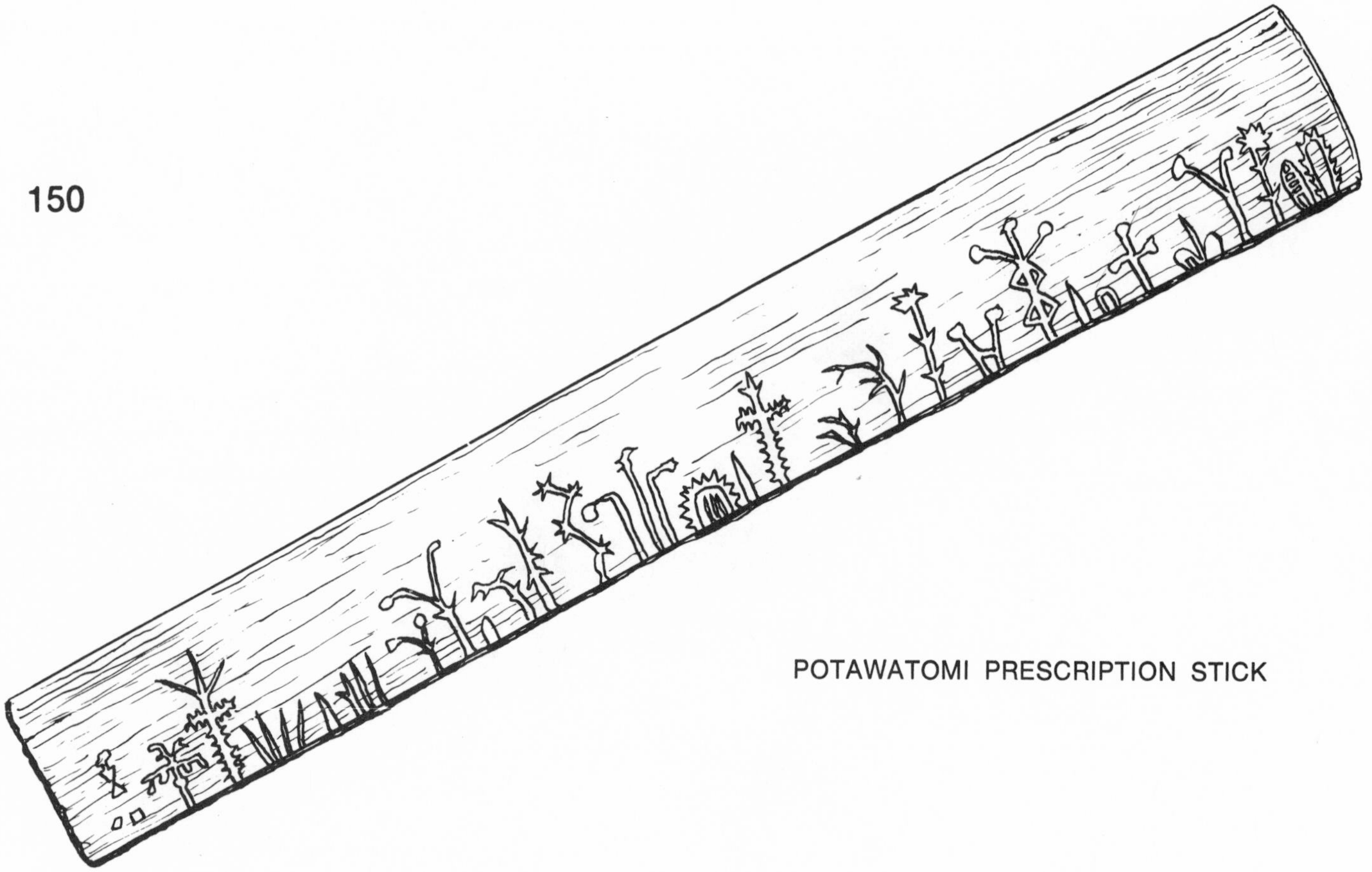

150

POTAWATOMI PRESCRIPTION STICK

SAUK

ALGONQUIAN STOCK

152

KEY

1. Supposed initial location and traditional domain of the Sauk.
2. Door County location.
3. Location at the mouth of the Fox River.
4. Approximate location of the "Great Town of the Saukies."

SYNONYMOUS NAMES USED IN REFERENCE TO THE SAUK

Asaukees	Sagaseys	Saukies
Hvattoehronon	Saginaw	Sawkis
Osagi	Sakawes	Saxes
Osaki	Sakes	Scungsicks
Osaugeeg	Saki	Shakies
Ouatoieronon	Saks	Shockeys
Ousaki	Saky	Shougheys
Ousakiouek	Saques	Skakies
Saasskies	Sauckeys	Socks
Sacks	Saucs	Taukies
Sacky	Saugies	Zake
Sacs	Saukees	

SAUK

The Sauk (literally, "people of the yellow earth," or "people of the outlet") were traditionally located in the Saginaw Bay region on the eastern side of the lower peninsula of Michigan. The name *Saginaw* signifies "the place of the Sauk." It is believed they occupied the whole of the Saginaw River Valley and its tributaries, spreading from Thunder Bay on the north to the head of the Shiawassee River on the south and Lake Michigan on the west to Detroit on the east.

The remainder of Michigan was occupied by the Potawatomi and the Lake Superior area was then occupied by the Ottawa and Chippewa. The Sauk seemd to be constantly at war with their Chippewa neighbors on the north, the Potawatomi on the south and the Neutrals in Canada. After a war council was held between the Chippewa, Potawatomi, Ottawa, and the Neutral tribes, they surprised the Sauk, massacring many of them.

Jerome Lallement, a Jesuit missionary, mentions in the 1644 *Relations,* that in the summer of 1642 the Neutrals with a force of two thousand warriors entered into the domain of the "Nation de Feu" and attacked a village of this tribe that was surrounded by palisades and defended by nine hundred staunch warriors. The village withstood for ten days a siege by their attackers, but many of the warriors were killed in the process. About eight hundred men, women, and children were taken captive after the village fell. Seventy of these, the finest warriors among them, were burned alive at the stake. While they were burning, the captors put out the eyes and cut away the lips of all the old men, leaving them to die in their agony.

Algonquian legend relates that the Sauk were forced out of this territory by bands of Chippewa and possibly Neutrals. The Sauk retreated beyond Lake Michigan and settled on Door County Peninsula between Green Bay and Lake Michigan. For a time they lived here in peace, but soon, because of their aggressiveness, came into violent conflict with their neighbors, the Menominee. The Menominee, although fewer in number, eventually forced the Sauk to retreat from the peninsula to an area at the mouth of the Fox River and southward.

The Sauk as an individual tribe was first mentioned in

the *Jesuit Relations* of 1640, by the Huron name of *Hvat-toehronon,* meaning "people of the sunset" or more briefly, "westerners." The first person to describe the Sauk was Father Allouez, a Jesuit missionary. He wrote in 1667 that the Sauk were more savage than any of the other Indians he had seen and that they were a numerous tribe, even though they moved about so much. He preached to roving bands of Sauk and Fox that visited near Chequamegon on Lake Superior.

Neither the Sauk nor the Fox accepted the intrusion of the French into their territories. The Menominee and Winnebago were allies and joined forces with the French to defeat their common enemies again. The Sauk gradually retreated south-

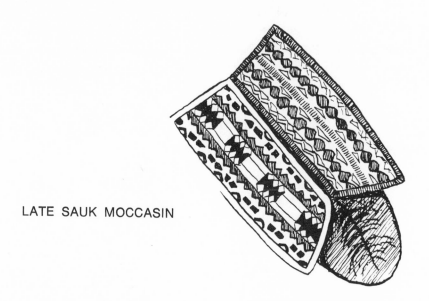

LATE SAUK MOCCASIN

ward and westward from the harassment of these three foes.

The Sauk, during the Pontiac Conspiracy, took part in the infamous game of lacrosse at Michilimackinac in 1763, in which the Sauk were to play the Chippewa. The strategy of the Indians was to flip the ball inside the stockade and then pursue it. The English soldiers, suspecting nothing, enjoyed watching the game. The squaws, standing nearby as spectators, concealed tomahawks under their blankets and handed them to the players 'as they rushed into the fort to massacre the garrison.

Jonathan Carver, born in Massachusetts, was the first Englishman to explore the area of Minnesota. He describes an early Sauk village in 1766: "On the 8th of October we

OLD SAUK INDIAN

SAUK CHIEFTAIN

got our canoes into the Ouisconsin River [Wisconsin], which at this place is more than a hundred yardswide; and the next day arrived at the Great Town of the Saukies. This is the largest and best built Indian town I ever saw. It contains about ninety houses, each large enough for several families. These are built of hewn plank neatly jointed, and covered with bark so compactly as to keep out the most penetrating rains. Before the doors are placed comfortable sheds, in which the inhabitants sit, when the weather will permit, and smoak their pipes. The streets are regular and spacious; so that it appears more like a civilized town than the abode of Savages. The land near the town is very good. In their plantations, which lie adjacent to their houses, and which are neatly laid out, they raise great quantities of Indian corn, beans, melons, &c. so that this place is esteemed the best market for traders to furnish themselves with provisions, of any within eight hundred miles of it."

Peter Pond mentions in his journal of 1773-1775, about the habits and customs of the Sauk. "These people are called Saukies. They are of a good size and well disposed — less inclind to tricks and bad manners than their neighbors. They will take of the traders goods on credit in the fall for their use. In winter and except for accident they pay the dept very well for Indians. I might have said inlightened or civilized Indians which are in general made worse by the operation."

The Sauk supported the English during the Revolution. The Rock River Sauk aided Great Britain in 1812. In 1804 and again in 1816 they ceded their lands.

In 1814, Col. George Hunt describes a Sauk hair cut. "That afternoon I witnessed a novel ceremony performed on a Sac Indian, no less than dispossessing him of a heavy head of hair by plucking him as we would pick a hen. They commenced by placing a quantity of ashes from our fire in two piles, leaving space for him who they were to operate on between the two piles. An Indian on each side knelt down, placing one hand each on the side of his head and soon every hair was pulled out except on the top, a sort of coxcomb was left and that was fixed with much care and painted with vermillion. All the time of the performance they cracked jokes with the fellow who stood it seemingly without pain, laughed and joked in turn. After they had finished, he jumped up, shook his blanket and walked off, not without a good dram of whisky from Blondo. This he had performed out of respect for a deceased wife. He was now at liberty to marry again."

Under the provisions of the treaty with the chiefs of the Sauk and Fox signed at Prairie du Chien, July 15, 1830, the land east of the Mississippi River was ceded to the United States. Black Hawk, a famous chief of the Sauk and Fox Indians, refused to acknowledge the treaty. In 1831 he and his followers attacked some Illinois villages and were driven off by the militia under General Gaines in June of that same year. The next spring Black Hawk returned with many

158

OTTAWA AND SAUK DUEL

LEGENDARY SPIRIT OF THE SAUK

warriors to attack the whites. General Scott marched United States troops against him. He defeated Black Hawk at the Wisconsin River on July 21, 1832, and again at the Bad Axe River on August 2 of the same year, bringing about the end of the Black Hawk War. During this war the 450 mounted Sauk warriors raised havoc with the U.S. Cavalry.

In 1833, John T. Irving, author of *Indian Sketches*, describes a Sauk brave and his dress. "I had formed but a poor opinion of the race from those whom I had already seen, but this was a princely fellow. He stood unmoved as we came up, viewing us with a calm, cold, but unwavering gaze. A large blanket, here and there streaked with vermilion, and ornamented with hawks' bells, was so disposed around his folded arms that it left bare his finely-formed shoulder and half of his high, sinewy chest. A bright steel-headed tomahawk peeped from beneath its folds, and a quiver of arrows hung at his back. His legs were cased in leggins of dressed deer-skin, with the edges cut into a rough fringe. He wore a pair of moccasins of dressed buffalo hide. The top of his head was closely shaven, and covered with vermilion, but his face was free from any coloring whatever, with the exception of a ring of black paint, which was carefully drawn around each eye."

The Potawatomi, Nation of the Fork, and the Sauk were all referred to as *Asistagueronon* ("People of the Place of Fire"), which is the tribal name of the Potawatomi. This fact makes it very difficult to distinguish these tribes from each other on early maps and in early writings.

The population of this tribe was first recorded in 1650, when the Sauk numbered approximately thirty-five hundred. In 1834 they were numbered at about twenty-five hundred.

They worshiped a great spirit, whom they acknowledged as the maker of heaven and earth, who dwells in the country toward the east. Manitos ("spirits," good or bad) are depicted in Sauk mythology and religion and are represented in the whole of nature as humans, birds, animals, fishes, reptiles, insects, plants, water, fire.

IROQUOIAN STOCK

ERIE

IROQUOIAN STOCK

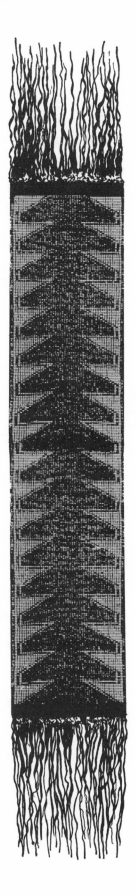

KEY

Shaded section indicates the approximate area of the Erie domain in the seventeenth century.

SYNONYMOUS NAMES USED IN REFERENCE TO THE ERIE

Cat Indians	Erieckronois	Kakwas
Cat Nation	Erieehronons	Nation des Chats
Cat Tribe	Eves	Nation of the Cat
Ehriehronnons	Heries	Rigneronnons
Erians		

ERIE

The name *Erie* probably signifies "people of the panther" or "people of the cat." Louis Hennepin, in his book, *A New Discovery,* 1698, mentions that the Iroquois gave Lake Erie its name by calling it *Erie Tejochavontiong.* The Huron Indians later called it *Lake Erige,* or *Erike,* which means "Lake of the Cat." Gabriel Sagard believed that the Erie were referred to as *Cat Tribe* because of the number of wildcats and lions that roamed in their country. He also thought that their robes, made from skins and with a number of animals' tails fringing the edges and at the back of the neck, may have had some significance.

In the seventeenth century they resided in the area extending south from the south shore of Lake Erie possibly to the Ohio River. An article in the *Jesuit Relations* of 1640-41, says that the territory of the Erie and their allies joined the Neutral Nation at the end of Lake Erie. According to legend the Erie warred with the Iroquois Nation many times before the Europeans arrived.

The Erie warriors were considered brave and courageous, never running away from a good fight. They used bows and poisoned arrows in battle and could shoot eight to ten arrows in the time it took to reload a musket.

In 1653 the Cat Nation (Erie) sent thirty ambassadors to the Seneca to renew their existing peace. One of the Erie

ANCIENT STONE AX

ERIE TRIBESMAN

Indians accidentally killed a Seneca which so enraged the Seneca Indians that they killed twenty-five of the Erie ambassadors in revenge. This incident was the beginning of the final war with the Iroquois. The Erie then attacked and burned a Seneca village. They also caught an Iroquois war party which probably was returning from the Great Lakes area, destroying their rear guard of eighty elite warriors. Some of the Erie scouts captured Annencraos, a great leader of the Iroquois, and carried him away. The Iroquois, in turn, raised eighteen hundred warriors to avenge those of their tribe who had been captured and killed and to punish the Erie for this humiliating experience. This large war party surrounded Rique, one of the Erie fortresses, and in spite of stiff resistance by approximately three to four thousand warriors, it was taken. By 1656 the Erie nation was totally destroyed except for about six hundred who surrendered to the Iroquois. The Iroquois had suffered many casualties, too, and were compelled to stay in Erie country for two months after the end of the battle to care for their casualties and recoup their losses as much as possible before returning to their own country with their Erie captives, some of whom they adopted, others of whom they possibly tortured.

168

HURON AND JESUIT

areas on the north bank of the St. Lawrence River northward, bordered by the Saguenay River on the east and Georgian Bay on the west; along the south side of the Bay of Gaspé, bordered on the west by the domain of the League of the Iroquois; and also on the east side of Lake Champlain and its tributaries.

The Iroquois received firearms from the Dutch, and by the year 1643 they had in their possession approximately four hundred guns. The Huron had very few firearms. This and the smallpox epidemic that decimated their people played an important role in their weak resistance against their well-armed Iroquois foe.

In July of 1648 the Iroquois attacked Huron villages on the frontier and the village of St. Joseph in Ontario. In March of 1649 they attacked St. Ignace and St. Louis in Ontario, capturing many of the Huron. These major defeats

WAR CLUB

demoralized the tribes, causing the small remnant to retreat in utter confusion, some to the Tobacco Nation directly west of them, some to the Erie on the southern shores of Lake Erie, and still others to various French settlements. The remainder of the Rock tribe were later persuaded to join the Onondaga Iroquois, and the Bear tribe was adopted into the Mohawk Iroquois tribe, while the Cord tribe remained loyal to the French. In 1653 there were more than one thousand Huron among the Onondaga tribe alone. The numbers among the other four Iroquois tribes is not known.

The Huron who had escaped to the Tobacco Indians were forced to retreat once more in 1649 when the Iroquois attacked the palisaded villages of the Tobacco Indians. The

HURON WAR CANOE

survivors, including the Huron refugees, retreated to St. Marie II on Christian Island, a few miles from the mainland in Georgian Bay. It is believed that this is the group that later became known as the Wyandotte. Here they suffered starvation during the winter and some, attempting to cross the ice to the mainland, perished when the ice broke beneath them.

Fear of the Iroquois war parties that were on the march throughout Huronia seeking the remaining Huron survivors forced them to evacuate this island. Most of the Indians at St. Marie II fled to Michilimackinac. After only a short time they were forced once more to flee from the Iroquois, this time to Manitoulin Island. Again they were forced to move, this time to Potawatomi Island near the entrance of Green Bay, Wisconsin, where the Ottawa and their allies had sought refuge. Later they moved westward about twenty miles, where they stayed with the Potawatomi. At this time they numbered approximately five hundred men, women, and children.

Fearing retaliation by their countrymen because they had massacred an Iroquois scouting party, they moved again. Some traveled to Orleans Island in the St. Lawrence River just above Quebec; the rest migrated southwest to the country of the Illinois on the Mississippi River. Here the Huron Indians acquired a new enemy, the Dakota, who in a short time made them withdraw to the source of the Black River in Wisconsin, where they were encountered in 1660. Later they settled at Chequamegon Bay near an Ottawa village. The Dakota persisted in their attacks on the Huron and Ottawa villages with such great success that they made them move back to the protection of the French settlements. In 1666 the French made peace with the Iroquois and by so doing made it possible for the Huron to move back to Michilimackinac about 1670. Here, near the location where Jacques Marquette had established the St. Ignace Mission, they built a village with a palisade around it.

Later some of the tribe migrated to Sandusky, Ohio, some to Detroit, and some across the Detroit River to Sandwich, Ontario. It was at these locations that they finally became known as the *Wyandotte*. They held title to a large part of Ohio and only by their permission were the Delaware and Shawnee tribes allowed to settle there. In 1721 a band of Wyandotte occupied the west banks of Lake Erie and Lake St. Clair.

W. KUBIAK

HURON HUNTER

The Huron took part in all the Indian military actions in the Great Lakes area and the Ohio Valley and were staunch allies of the British in opposing the Americans. When peace finally came in 1815, they received a large parcel of land in Michigan and Ohio, of which they sold a large portion under a treaty in 1819. They kept a small portion near Upper Sandusky, Ohio, and one on the Huron River near Detroit. These tracts were sold in 1842 and the Huron tribe was relocated in Wyandotte County, Kansas, then later to a small area in northeastern Oklahoma.

Gabriel Sagard, a Recollet historian, described the Huron villages in 1623-1624 as follows, "There are about 20 or 25 towns and villages, of which some are not at all shut, nor closed, and others are fortified with long pieces of timber in triple ranks, interlaced one with another to the height of a long pike [approximately sixteen feet] and reenforced on the inside with broad, coarse strips of bark, eight or nine feet in height; below there are large trees, with their branches lopped off, laid lengthwise on very short trunks of trees, forked at one end, to keep them in place; then above these stakes and bulwarks there are galleries or platforms, called 'ondaqua,' which are furnished with stones to be hurled against an enemy in time of war, and with water to extinguish any fire which might be kindled against them. Persons ascend to these by means of ladders quite poorly made and difficult, which are made of long pieces of timber wrought by many hatchet strokes to hold the foot firm in ascending." He also mentions that they carried large shields and wore greaves on the legs and cuirasses made from boughs that were held together with interwoven cords. Champlain gives a similar account of their dress.

The Huron men were well proportioned, and taller, as a rule, than the Frenchmen. Their faces were painted in various pigments native to their land. These were mixed with bear grease or sunflower oil as a base. Their faces had sharper features and were longer than the Algonquian's. They had high cheekbones, hooked noses, very white-looking teeth, bronze-colored skin, and straight black hair that they kept highly greased. The majority of the warriors removed a good portion of their hair as did the Iroquois. Their bodies and faces were usually hairless from birth, unlike the average European. During warm weather they wore only a breech cloth and, if needed, leggings. The men's duties were fighting, hunting, fishing, trading, witch-doctoring, and the building of longhouses and canoes. The squaws performed all the household duties, worked the fields, gathered firewood, tanned hides for clothing, made pottery, and carried all the supplies and equipment on journeys. Their hair was greased flat to their heads and hung down in a braid that was usually tied with a dried eel or snakeskin. The women wore little clothing in the summer, most of them wrapping a short skirt similar to a kilt about their hips and thighs. They loved ornaments and graced themselves with long strings of beads made from shells and bones. For winter they wore robes made of woven strips of rabbit fur.

"The Feast of the Dead" was a burial ritual held every ten or twelve years by the Huron Indians. They took the bodies of the deceased from high platforms where they had been kept and removed all the remaining flesh and cleaned and polished the bones. They then began to mourn the dead, later carrying the bones in beaver pelts to a large communal burial pit where, after feasting for three days, they placed the bones beside the bones of those previously buried.

Over a hundred of these burial pits have been found in Northern Simcoe. From one such pit at Ossossane, nine miles south of Midland, in Tiny Township, Ontario, the bones of over seven hundred Huron Indians were unearthed.

In 1615 the Huron population was estimated to be between 20,000 and 35,000. It is believed that in 1648 they numbered about 20,000. In 1736 there were about 1,300; in 1748, between 500 and 850. In 1812 only about 1,000 Huron Indians survived.

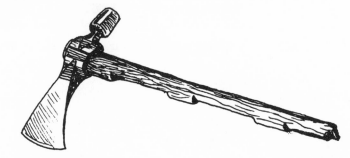

TRADE AX

180

181

HURON WOMAN AND CHILD, 1600

W. KUBIAK

IROQUOIS

IROQUOIAN STOCK

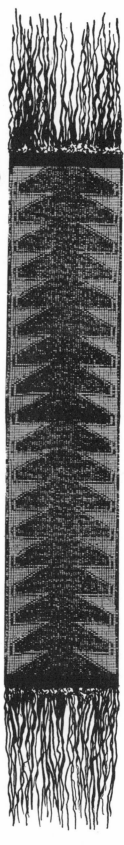

KEY

1. Mohawk territory.
2. Oneida territory.
3. Onondaga territory.
4. Cayuga territory.
5. Seneca territory.
6. Lands assigned to the Tuscarora by the Oneida, which were bounded by the Unadilla, the Chenango, and the Susquehanna rivers.

SYNONYMOUS NAMES USED IN REFERENCE TO THE IROQUOIS

Acquinoshioni	Five Nations	Nadowaig
Cannassoone	Hiroquois	Natuagi
Canton Indians	Hotinnonchiendi	Naudoway
Confederate Indians	Ironois	Six Nations
Confederate Nations	Massawonacks	Yroquois
Five Indian Cantons	Mingos	

IROQUOIS

The term *Iroquois* is a French corruption of a name which in its original form in the Algonkin tongue meant "real adders." The Iroquois in their own tongue called themselves by a term that meant "original men" or "men of men."

Some historians contend that the Iroquois originally came to the New York area from the south and west around the turn of the fourteenth century. When first known to the Europeans, the Iroquois were a confederacy or league comprised of five tribes. There is a legend that Deganawidah, an Iroquois prophet, and Hiawatha, his disciple, were the founders of this confederation. However, Deganawidah is

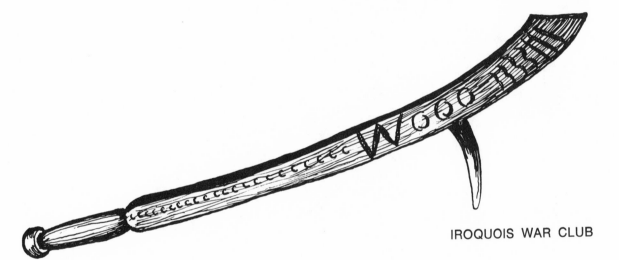

IROQUOIS WAR CLUB

supposed to have lived during the middle of the fifteenth century while Hiawatha is reputed to have lived during the middle of the sixteenth century.

It is presumed that the league when first formed, possibly in 1570 during a war with the Huron and certain other Algonquian tribes, consisted only of three Iroquoian tribes, the Seneca, Onondaga, and the Mohawk, and that the Oneida and the Cayuga were adopted or accepted into the league later because the Oneida conceded that the Mohawk were their fathers, while the Cayuga believed the Seneca to be theirs.

The Mohawk, whose name means "man eaters," called themselves "the possessors of the flint." They were more hostile than the other tribes in the league. The Oneida,

186

IROQUOIS WARRIOR, 1609

W.KUBIAK

whose name means "people of the standing stone," were called *Onneyette* by the Dutch. *Onondaga* means "the people of the hills," probably derived from the fact that their village, called by the same name and considered the capital city of the league, was situated on top of a hill. *Cayuga* means "people of the mucky land." Many of this tribe moved to Canada after the American Revolution. The Seneca, whose name means "the great hill people," were probably the largest tribe of the league and were the most aggressive in warfare against the Huron who inhabited the country adjacent to them.

When the Europeans first contacted the Iroquois, they inhabited the territory from the east watershed of Lake Champlain to the west watershed of the Genesee River and from the Adirondacks to the land of the Conestoga, an Iroquoian tribe that formerly resided on the Susquehanna River and its tributaries.

In 1722 the Tuscarora were admitted to this confederacy and from that time on it was known as the League or Confederacy of Six Nations.

During early summer of 1609 an event took place that was to have lasting consequences and cause a prolonged and bloody conflict between the Iroquois on the one hand and the French with their Indian allies on the other. Samuel de Champlain decided to further the cause of the Ottawa Algonkin Indians, who were friends of the Huron. He left Quebec with eleven Frenchmen and a flotilla of canoes loaded with Indians to attack the Iroquois nation. About three-quarters of the Indians deserted the expedition early in the trip because of a dispute, and all but two of his Frenchmen were sent back to Quebec. With only about sixty Indians following him, he proceeded on his journey into unknown country. He discovered the lake that now bears his name and on these shores he met the Iroquois. Champlain, in his steel breastplate, his matchlock in hand and his small band of Indian followers, waited for the attack by some two hundred of the fiercest warriors in the New World. When the Iroquois charged they met a resounding discharge from Chaplain's matchlock. Three of them were wounded or killed. The use of lightning and thunder to combat his enemies proved too much for the superstitious minds of the Iroquois and they retreated. Many were killed and a few were captured to be tortured by the Algonkin Indians. This expedition made the Iroquois

W. KUBIAK

SENECA

189

MOHAWK

W. KUBIAK

bitter enemies of the French and closer allies of the British until the close of the French regime in Canada in 1763.

In 1657 there were about twenty-four Iroquois villages. After they conquered the Erie, a tribe of Iroquoian stock who lived on the south shore of Lake Erie, they extended their borders west to Lake Erie. Subsequently they established settlements on the upper Allegheny and Susquehanna rivers and also on the north banks of Lake Ontario. In 1750 they had approximately fifty villages.

The population seemed to fluctuate greatly at different times; their constant hostilities against enemy nations greatly reduced their numbers from time to time. It is believed that they numbered about 2,250 warriors in 1689, but these

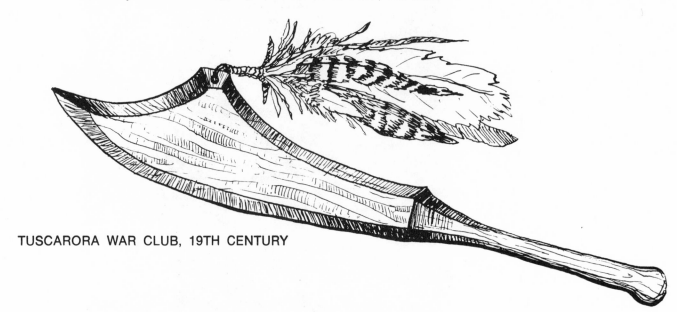

TUSCARORA WAR CLUB, 19TH CENTURY

were reduced by war, disease, and other reasons to about only 1,230 warriors in 1698. They made up for a good share of their casualites by adopting into their tribe a chosen number of the enemies they had captured alive. The remainder, however, were tortured unmercifully until they died.

The custom of adoption was so widespread that at one period the adopted members equaled or outnumbered the true Iroquois. It is very possible that there are Indians today who believe they are full-blooded Iroquois who do not have any Iroquois blood in them. During the last quarter of the seventeenth century the Iroquois attained a population of about ten thousand. In the eighteenth century their number was estimated between ten and twelve thousand.

Although the Iroquois did not live in Michigan, they were responsible for a great deal of the movement and relocation of the tribes about the Great Lakes. The Iroquois received firearms from the Dutch in trade for furs. This enabled them to conquer most of the tribes from the Ottawa to the Tennessee rivers between the Kennebec River and Lake Michigan and down the Illinois River. The Chippewa forestalled their penetration to the west, while to the north they were warded off somewhat by the French and their Indian allies.

When the American Revolution broke out, the Iroquois decided not to enter it as a confederation but to allow each tribe to decide on a course of action. The Mohawk, Onondaga, Cayuga, Seneca, and about half of the Tuscarora decided to take sides with the British. After the Revolution ended in 1781 the Iroquoian tribes who had helped the British were settled on a reservation on the Grand River in Ontario by the Canadian government. Nearly all of the Iroquois who remained in the United States were settled on reservations in the state of New York. Only the Oneida

SENECA MASK

W. KUBIAK

CUYUGA

193

ONEIDA

W. KUBIAK

194

IROQUOIS WOMAN

W. Kubiak '61

tribe was placed on a reservation near Green Bay, Wisconsin.

During the seventeenth century, the Iroquois wore a type of armor which included bucklers and breastplates believed to be made of wooden sprigs laced with a type of fibre which Samuel de Champlain believed to be made of cotton. Some of the warriors carried shields, and the chiefs or leaders wore tall feathers on their heads. Before going into battle they painted their faces with red, black, or other colors in the style suited to the individual warrior's taste. This was a sacred custom.

Most Iroquois removed the hair from every part of the head except for a tuft on the crown usually referred to as the

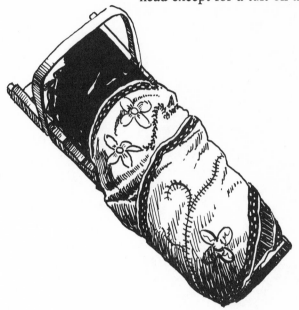

IROQUOIS CRADLEBOARD

scalplock. This they cherished very dearly. Some removed only part of their hair, resulting in the famous Mohawk hairdo. As decorations, tattooed figures of birds, animals and reptiles and many forms of designs were also popular with these Indians.

In the winter they wore beaver robes, even covering the head with them when it was very cold. Separate sleeves that were fastened together across the shoulders with sinew were used.

Claude Chauchetiere (1645-1709), a Jesuit missionary, in a letter dated 1682, describes a group of Christian Iroquois: "The women have no other head dress than their hair, which they part over the middle of the head, and then tie

196

TUSCARORA

W. KUBIAK

197

ONONDAGA

W. KUBIAK

behind with a sort of ribbon, which they make out of eel-skin painted a bright red. I myself have often been deceived, and have taken it for a real ribbon. They grease their hair, which thereby becomes as black as jet. As for the men, they are ridiculous in dressing their hair, and there is not one who does not do it up in a special fashion. On Sundays and Feast-days, the men and women wear fine white chemises; and the women take wonderful care to clothe themselves so modestly that there is nothing indecorous or uncovered about them, for they closely fasten the chemise. This falls over a petticoat, consisting of a blue or red blanket, a brasse [about six feet] or more square, which they fold in two, and simply gird around the waist; the chemise, which falls over this sort of petticoat, reaches only to the knees. . . . On other days they are poorly but modestly clad."

NEUTRALS

IROQUOIAN STOCK

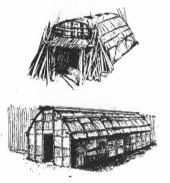

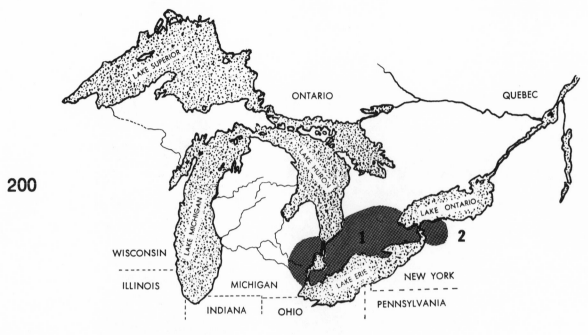

200

KEY

1. Shaded area indicates the approximate habitat of the Neutral Nation.
2. Neutral Indians were captured and adopted by the Seneca.

SYNONYMOUS NAMES USED IN REFERENCE TO THE NEUTRALS

Aondiron	Attenonderonk	Neuters
Atiaonrek	Attinoindarons	Neutral Nation
Atiouendaronk	Attiwandaronk	Neutre
Atiraguenrek	Nation Neuht	Ongniaahraronon
Atirhagenrenrets	Neuter Nation	Rhagenratka

NEUTRALS

The Neutral Indians were known as the *Attiwandaronk* by the Huron Indians. The word means, "They are the people who speak a slightly different language." Later they were nicknamed *Neutrals* by the French because of their neutrality in the Huron and Iroquois wars. The Neutrals were actually a confederation of Aondiron and Ongniaahraronon. The Wenrohronon joined them later.

In the seventeenth century they inhabited the area north of Lake Erie, their domain extending east from the Niagara River (then called the *River of the Neutrals* or the *Onguiaaha River*) into what is now the state of New York. Their area extended west across the St. Clair and Detroit rivers for a distance unknown. In 1626 they were visited by a Recollet Friar, Joseph de La Roche Daillon, who reported that there was a large population residing in twenty-eight villages of substantial size and many smaller ones.

The Neutral Nation was at war with the Mascouten and other western tribes during the years around 1640. At this time they sent a large war party of about two thousand warriors against the "Nation du feu" (Mascouten and Illinois ?). They attacked a palisaded village which was defended by approximately nine hundred warriors who stood their ground for ten days and nights, after which the Neutrals stormed the palisades and were able to capture eight hundred of the enemy, killing or routing the remainder. The population of the Neutrals at this time is estimated to have been about twelve thousand, who lived in approximately forty villages.

In 1647 an Iroquois warrior on a mission to commit murder among the Tionontati (Tobacco) Indians was captured and put to death by the Huron Indians. The Huron lived among the Neutrals at this time and in revenge the Iroquois destroyed one of the Neutral villages, taking several captives. This, of course, broke the existing neutrality between the tribes, but the Neutrals tried to recover their captives by peaceful means rather than to risk war, hoping they would be able to avenge their losses at a more advantageous time.

In 1649 the Neutral Nation could see that the Hurons were near extinction, due to the many defeats they had suffered from the Iroquois. Wanting to gain favor with the

202

EARLY NEUTRAL TRIBESMAN

W. KUBIAK

victor rather than the vanquished, the Neutrals captured all of the Huron fugitives who had sought refuge in their villages. Their only reward, however, was successive attacks by the Iroquois. In 1650 and 1651 they were totally subdued and taken captive, most of them being adopted by the Seneca tribe in what is now the state of New York.

The Neutrals had a very strange custom practiced by none of the other Indian tribes. It is said that they would kill every animal they came across, even though they did not need it for food or pelts, because they believed the animal would warn others of its kind, making it next to impossible to find them when they needed them for food or clothing.

WAR CLUB

When mourning for a loved one, the Neutral Indians would blacken both their faces and that of the deceased. They would decorate the dead body with feathers and other regalia and often tattoo it with symbols and designs. When one of their members was killed in warfare, the chief, over the remains of the deceased, would urge the close friends and relatives to avenge their loved one's death.

They are said to have surpassed the Huron Indians in form and stature. Their language was somewhat similar to that of the Huron, but their customs and manners were almost identical.

During the summer months the men of the tribe wore no clothing. They were tattooed on the head and body with a powder made from charcoal. The Neutrals were not considered as adept at handling the canoe as were their neighbors, the Huron.

204

NEUTRAL WITH CANOE

W. KUBIAK '61

TIONONTATI

IROQUOIAN STOCK

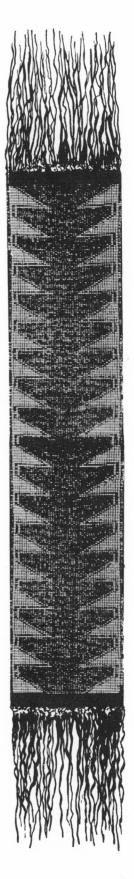

KEY

1. Shaded area indicates the approximate location of the early Tionontati territory.
2. Approximate location of Potawatomi mission in 1658, to which the Tionontati fled.
3. Location of fugitive Tionantati remnant during 1660.
4. The Tinontati join the Huron Indians at La Pointe.
5. 1670 location at Mackinac.
6. Detroit location up to 1721.

SYNONYMOUS NAMES USED IN REFERENCE TO THE TIONONTATI

Chenondadees	Nation du Petum	Tionnontates Hurons
Deer Clan	Nation of Tobacco	Tionnotante
Deonondadies	Petuneux	Tobacco Indians
Dionondes	Petun Indians	Tobacco Nation
Etionnontates	Quiennontateronons	Tuinontatek
Gens du Petun	Shawendadies	Wolf Clan
Jenundadees	Theonontateronons	Younondadys
Nation de Petun		

TIONONTATI

The Tionontati, which probably means "There the mountain stands," are generally known as the *Tobacco Indians* today. They lived in the Blue Mountains, south of Nottawasaga Bay in Grey and Simcoe Counties in Ontario. They bordered the Huron Nation. In early times the Tionontati and the Huron were enemies and waged bloody wars. Just before the Jesuits came to Huronia they made peace and formed an alliance against their common enemies. The French first came in contact with them in 1616 and referred to them as the *Nation du Petun* ("Nation of Tobacco"), because they raised enormous amounts of tobacco.

In 1640 the Tobacco Nation was a confederacy made up of two separate tribes or clans — the Deer Clan and the Wolf

CLAY PIPE

Clan. These two groups inhabited nine permanent villages which were similar to those of the Huron.

When the Huron were defeated by the Iroquois in 1649, many of the survivors fled to the Tobacco Nation who accepted the refugees. The Iroquois retaliated by sending a powerful war party to Etarita, one of their important villages. The warriors were away at the time and the village was taken completely by surprise. The dwellings were set on fire and a large number of the inhabitants were killed or taken captive. The remaining Tobacco Indians, with the

TIONONTATI STORYTELLER

Huron refugees, fled to an area southwest of Lake Superior. In 1658 there were approximately five hundred of these fugitives at the Potawatomi Mission near Green Bay, Wisconsin. In 1660 Pierre Radisson encountered another group in northeastern Illinois. They also were seeking refuge from the Iroquois. A short while later the group situated at Green Bay moved again, joining the Huron Indians at La Pointe in Wisconsin. In 1670 both of these tribes were residing at Mackinac, Michigan. Soon the Tobacco Indians completely merged with the Hurons and were recognized as the Wyandotte. Up to 1721 they were still dwelling in

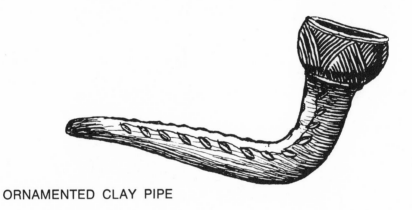

ORNAMENTED CLAY PIPE

the Detroit area and were recognized as *Tionontati Huron*.

The Tobacco Indians spoke the same language as the Huron. In addition, however, in two of their villages they spoke Algonquian. Their customs resembled those of the Huron and they dressed much as the Huron did.

TIONONTATI WOMAN, 1600

WENROHRONON

IROQUOIAN STOCK

KEY

1. Shaded area indicates approximate territory occupied by the Wenrohronon in 1639.
2. Area in Neutral territory to which they fled for protection from the Iroquois.
3. Moved from Neutral territory to Huronia in 1639.
4. A number of the Wenrohronon were captured and sent back to the Seneca domain where most of them were adopted into the Seneca tribe.

SYNONYMOUS NAMES USED IN REFERENCE TO THE WENROHRONON

Ahouenrochrhonons	Oenronronnons	Weanohronons
Awenrehronon	Ouenro Nation	Wenro
Conestoga		

WENROHRONON

The name *Wenrohronon* signifies "the inhabitants of the place of floating scum." This tribe, closely linked with the Neutral Nation, in 1639 resided on their eastern borders, which probably placed them between the Neutral and Iroquoian territories or to the west or southwest of them. They were an important tribe, numbering from twelve hundred to two thousand before warfare with the Iroquois decimated their numbers. They were one of four associate Iroquoian tribes living south of Lake Erie, the others being the Erie, the Conestoga, and the "People of Wyoming Valley."

For some reason, the Neutrals severed their close relationship with the Wenrohronon and left them defenseless against the looming threat of the Iroquois. Their only alternative was to ask for protection from the Huron Nation. They welcomed them and even offered warriors to escort

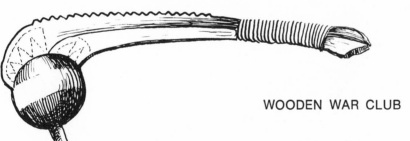

WOODEN WAR CLUB

them to their country, probably because they felt the Wenrohronon would help bolster the defense of the Huron Nation. Over six hundred Wenrohronon started this perilous journey of about 250 miles but many women and children died from the hardships encountered along the way. Upon arriving in Huronia they were suffering from an epidemic; even so, the Huron welcomed them into their dwellings. Later they were accepted as members into the tribe.

Some were captured by the Iroquois and were adopted and lived with the Seneca tribe. After five years passed, the chief of the refugees led a war party of over three hundred warriors.

Their language, dress, customs, and shelters were similar to those of the Neutral Nation.

W. KUBIAK

WENROHRONON HUNTSMAN

SIOUAN STOCK

ASSEGUNS

SIOUAN STOCK

KEY

1. Location prior to 1649.
2. Piqutinong location.
3. Grand River location.
4. Chicago, last known location.

SYNONYMOUS NAMES USED IN REFERENCE TO THE ASSEGUN

Assigunaigs   Bone Indians

ASSEGUN

Indian legend tells of a tribe of Indians known as *Assegun*, which means "Black Bass" in the Chippewa language. They were also referred to as *Bone Indians* and *Assigunaigs*. The Assegun are believed to be of the Siouan or Iroquoian linguistic stock, most probably the former. Many historians believe that the Sioux once occupied the upper peninsula of Michigan and were forced out by the Chippewa and possibly other enemy tribes.

The Assegun lived on the upper parts of Lake Huron prior to 1649. Their tribal seat was established on Mack-

WOOD HAFTED AX

inac Island; their territory extended over a fairly large portion of the eastern part of Michigan's upper peninsula, from the mouth of the St. Mary's River, south to the north shore of Lake Huron, west to Point St. Ignace and north and west along the shores and islands of Lake Michigan.

During the excursions into the Ottawa domain on the Manitoulin Islands, the Assegun killed some of the Ottawa people. The inevitable resulted — war. The Chippewa became allies of the Ottawa against the Assegun. The first battle took place near where the town of De Tour now stands. The Ottawa and Chippewa pursued the Assegun westward until the Assegun took to their canoes and crossed the strait to Piqutinong, where the French later built old Fort Michilimackinac. Here they settled, eventually building a village on the spot.

The Ottawa gradually moved from the Manitoulin Islands, and St. Ignace became their tribal seat. Again Assegun braves made excursions into Ottawa lands, this time killing an Ottawa woman who was planting corn. In revenge the Ottawa raised a war party to attack the Assegun village. Here they found only old men, women, and children. Upon learning that the warriors had gone up the Cheboygan River, they followed them and found the Assegun's canoes hidden under bushes overhanging the banks. Here they lay in wait. The surprise was complete and the Assegun were massacred. The few survivors retreated to the eastern shores of Lake Michigan, then later moved to the Grand River. During this time the Assegun were confederates of the Mascouten. Once again they retreated from their old enemies beyond the Grand River towards Chicago. Here they disappear from history. It is

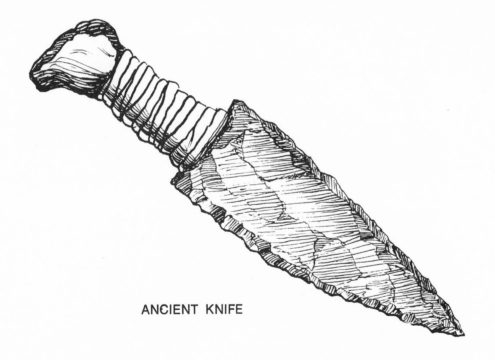

ANCIENT KNIFE

221

ASSEGUN WARRIOR

possible that they may have been assimilated into one of the Siouan tribes, such as the Winnebago.

Some authorities believe that the Assegun and Mascouten are one and the same tribe. However, since the Mascouten were of the Algonquian linguistic stock and the Assegun spoke a language not understood by the Algonquian tribes, this is highly improbable.

222

DAKOTA

SIOUAN STOCK

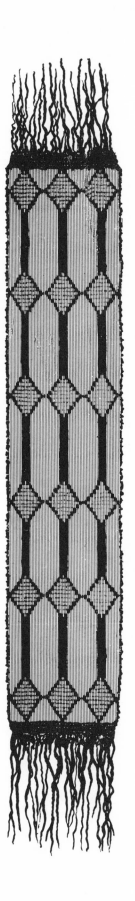

224

KEY

1. Approximate ancient legendary location of the Dakota.
2. First contact of the Dakota by the Chippewa at Sault Ste. Marie, according to legend.
3. Their approximate location in 1640.

SYNONYMOUS NAMES USED IN REFERENCE TO THE DAKOTA

Abboinug	Nadowessioux	Poualakes
Adouesis	Nadvesin	Roasters
Bwoinug	Nakota	Saoux
Dacota	Naudowessie	Siou
Dacotah	Nedowessioux	Sioux
Lakota	Nodowaysesug	Soo
Madowesians	Nottawessie	Wanak
Nadoweisiw		

DAKOTA

Today the Dakota are generally known as the Sioux. The Chippewa called them *Nadoweisiw,* which probably means "snake" or "enemy." The French corrupted this name to *Nadowessioux,* from which the name *Sioux* comes. Ancient legends say that the Dakota came from the northeast and were moving toward the southwest. Originally, then, they were from an area somewhere north of the Great Lakes. Their gradual westward movement was probably caused by attacks by the Chippewa and possibly other hostile tribes.

Chippewa legend says that they first came in contact with the Dakota at Sault Ste. Marie. The earliest extant historical mention of the Dakota is 1640. The *Jesuit Relations* of that year mentions that in the vicinity of the "Nation des Puans" (Winnebago) are the "Nadvesin" (Dakota), "Assinipour" (Assiniboin). In the *Relations* of 1642, mention is made of the fact that "the adouesis [Dakota] are living 18 days journey to the northwest" or

SIOUX WAR CLUB

west of Sault Ste. Marie. Up to the eighteenth century, it is believed, the Dakota still had villages in some parts of northern Michigan and in Wisconsin. It is theorized by some that certain groups of the Siouan family became divided near the area where the Winnebago lived, by Green Bay and Lake Winnebago. From this locality they spread to several different areas, thus becoming distinct groups.

When they lived in the woodlands of the east they dwelt in wigwams made of bark and woven mats, but when they moved to the plains and prairies they lived in earth lodges and skin tipis. The Dakota depended chiefly on the buffalo (bison) as their main source of food. They held them in high religious esteem because of their importance as food.

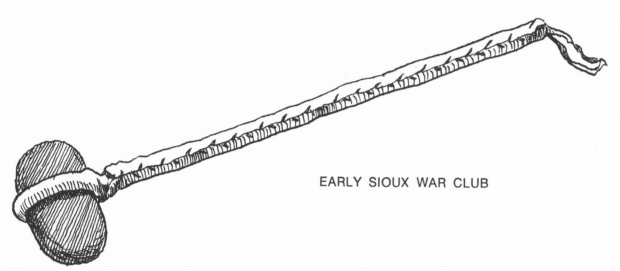

EARLY SIOUX WAR CLUB

In early times the only domestic animals they had were dogs, but later they were introduced to horses. This caused a major change in their way of life, enabling them to follow the migratory buffalo to wherever they were to be found in abundance. Their whole life thereafter depended on the horse and buffalo.

The Dakota are considered to be the highest caliber of all the Western Indian tribes. They were brave warriors who conquered or forced out all rival tribes with only one exception — the Chippewa.

Their numbers during the early years when they are believed to have resided in upper Michigan and in Wisconsin are not known.

DAKOTA, 1800

DAKOTA BRAVE

TUTELO

SIOUAN STOCK

KEY

1. The Tutelo Indians' legendary location on the Detroit and Rouge rivers.
2. Eighteenth century location of the Tutelo Indians at Shamokin.
3. Skogari location, 1748.
4. 1771 settlement on Cayuga Lake.
5. Grand River Reservation in Ontario.

SYNONYMOUS NAMES USED IN REFERENCE TO THE TUTELO

Kattera	Tiederigoene	Totiri
Shateras	Tiutei	Tuetle
Taderighrones	Toderichroone	Tutaloes
Tentilves	Tolera	Tutecoes
Teuteloe	Toleri	Tuttelee
Thedirighroonas	Totera	Yesah

TUTELO

The Tutelo are an eastern Siouan tribe who, along with the Nottoway and Meherrin, both Iroquoian tribes, formerly occupied the mountainous districts of Virginia.

The name *Tutelo* in the English language designates a certain tribe of Indians, but in Iroquoian it is a term used to describe all the Siouan tribes of Virginia and Carolina.

The Tutelo in the early eighteenth century, moved north and settled on the Susquehanna River at Shamokin, Pennsylvania, with the Iroquois as their protector. They did not move en masse to the land of the Iroquois, but rather in small groups or bands during a period of several years. During this slow migration they came in frequent contact with traders who gave them whiskey as a form of barter. This corrupted their characters and brought contempt and scorn to their kind. It was at this time that they lost all

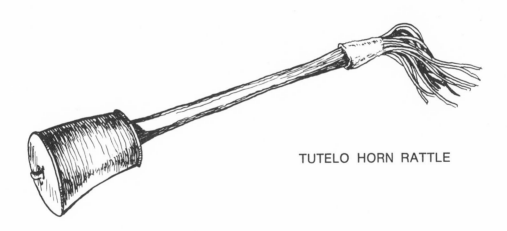

TUTELO HORN RATTLE

identity with their former culture and became forsaken itinerants.

Even so, the Iroquoian Nation thought very highly of the Tutelo as brave and daring warriors. They also used their settlements as refuge points while traversing this area in raids against the Cherokee and Catawba.

Later the Tutelo moved up the river to Skogari in Columbia County, Pennsylvania, and in 1771 they settled on the east side of Cayuga Lake in New York. This village, which was in Cayuga territory, was called Coreorgonel, and was later destroyed. The surviving Tutelo Indians moved to

232

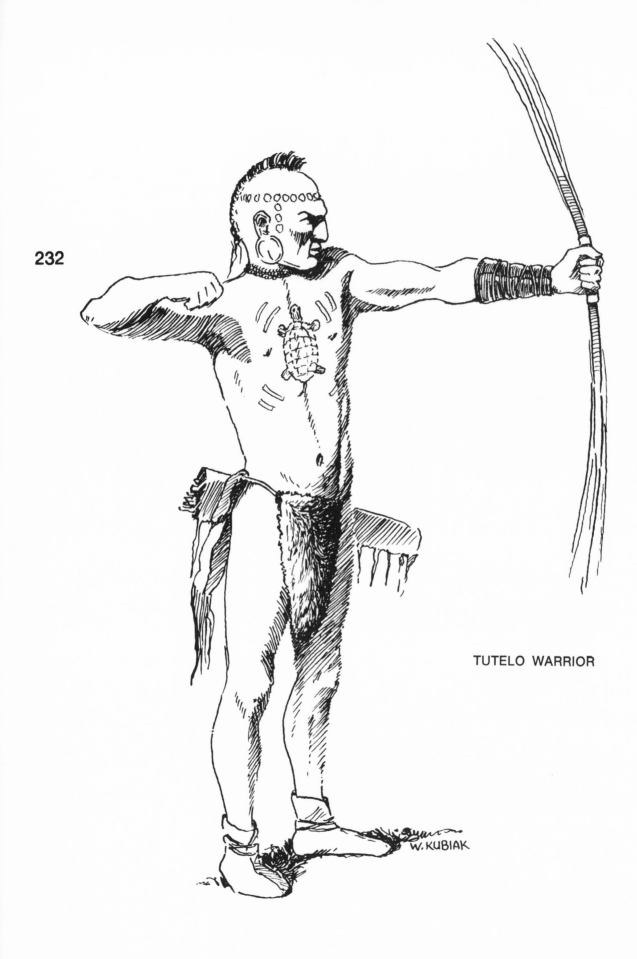

TUTELO WARRIOR

W. KUBIAK

Fort Niagara and from there to Canada, where they finally settled on a reservation near Brantford, Ontario.

Henry Gillman, of Detroit, in 1874, made this interesting commentary: "Indian tradition says that these mounds along our river were built in ancient times by a people of whom they (the Indians) know nothing, and for whom they have no name; that the mounds were occupied by the Tuetle Indians, and subsequently by the Wyandottes, but were constructed long before their time. These facts were ascertained by me in the course of some investigations which I made several years ago, and at that time I further learned that the Tuetle Indians had been absorbed by the Six Nations, and if any survive it is there they must be looked for.

"In this connection it is proper to state that I have lately been informed, through the instrumentality of Prof. Henry [Joseph, (1797-1878)], of the Smithsonian Institute, of the result of some inquiries made at my suggestion in regard to the name Tuetle. The conclusion arrived at is that the word Tuetle is probably a corruption of Tutelo, a tribe 'admitted as a younger member of the confederacy of the Six Nations, about the middle of the last century [1750]'; and that the Tuteloes 'are believed to have migrated from Virginia northward, to lands assigned them on the Susquehanna by the Six Nations; but very little is known of their early history and migrations.' An interesting paper on the Tuteloes was read by the Rev. J. Anderson, before the American Philological Association, in July 1871. Reporting Mr. H. Hale's discoveries, this assigns the Tuteloes to the Dakotan and not the Iroquois stock, and gives an account of Mr. Hale's visit to Kikungha, the last survivor of the tribe of the Tuteloes, and who has since died at the age of 106 years.

"The establishment of the identity of the Tuetles with the Tuteloes, and their residence on these mounds and along the Detroit River, is not only an interesting addition to our local history, but is of special value in view of its tending to sustain Mr. Hale's opinion (opposed to the conclusions of others regarding the Dakotan migration) that 'in former times the whole of what is now the central portion of the United States from the Mississippi nearly to the Atlantic, was occupied by Dakotan tribes, who have been cut up and gradually exterminated by the intrusive and more energetic Algonquins and Iroquois.'"

Thus the Tuetle Indians around the Detroit area may have been the same tribe as the Tutelo, or only a branch of this tribe. However, it is also possible that they were called Tuetles by the Iroquois, because they were of Siouian extraction, and were actually of another distinct Siouan tribe with separate identity such as the Winnebago.

The Tutelo were tall and robust Indians, with oval-shaped faces and large features. These people were tillers of the soil, relying on this mode of life extensively to exist. They were inclined to be warlike in nature. In 1763 their population was estimated to be between two and five hundred men, women, and children.

When they were settled at the Grand River Reservation near Brantford, Ontario, they intermarried with the Cayuga and Onondaga tribes to such a great degree that it is believed that there is not one Indian living today who is a full-blooded Tutelo, even though the tribe still exists in name.

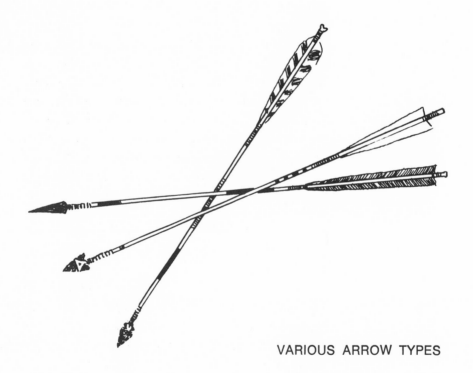

VARIOUS ARROW TYPES

WINNEBAGO

SIOUAN STOCK

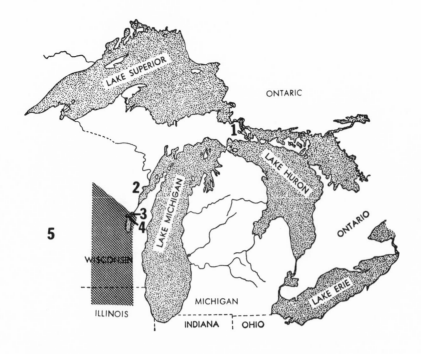

236

KEY

1. Possible early location.
2. First known location, 1634.
3. Location as shown on map published with Marquette's Journal, 1681.
4. Island location on "Winnebago Town," 1778.
5. Village location in 1832, La Crosse. Shaded area indicates approximate location of Winnebago holdings on Carver's map, 1766-1767.

SYNONYMOUS NAMES USED IN REFERENCE TO THE WINNEBAGO

Aoeatsioaenronnon	Nation of Stinkers	Puants
Banaboueks	Nipegon	Stinkers
Bay Indians	Otchagras	Winibagos
Hotcangara	Otonkah	Winnebager
Huchungara	Ouenibegouc	Winnebaygo
Mipegois	Ouininpigou	Winnepaus
Nation des Puans	Puans	Winnibigog

WINNEBAGO

Winnebago, in its corrupted version, means "people of the filthy water." They have been known to the Europeans since the year 1634, when they were found living on the shores of Green Bay, Wisconsin, by Jean Nicolet, a Frenchman. It is believed that at this time the Winnebago inhabited an area which extended all the way to Lake Winnebago. It is not known how long they had resided in this area before the arrival of the Europeans. There is a possibility that they, along with other Siouan tribes, were forced from an eastern or southern area at an earlier time.

Their closest neighbors were the Central Algonquians, whose different tribes surrounded them in the Green Bay area. They also were in constant touch with the Iowa, a kindred tribe who were closely related to the Oto and Missouri. All four of these Siouan tribes have dialect and cultural similarities. However, the culture and craftman-

WINNEBAGO BRAVE

ship of the Winnebago are closely knit with that of the Central Algonquian tribes surrounding them.

Early in the seventeenth century an alliance of Indian tribes attacked and greatly reduced the Winnebago population. Later, the Illinois attacked them, killing many and carrying the rest away captive. Subsequently all of the captives were released and allowed to return to their villages where they regrouped and formed a tribe once again.

According to the map published with Jacques Marquette's *Journal* of 1681, there was a Winnebago village, listed as *"Puans,"* located close to the north end of Lake Winnebago. It appears that the Winnebago had moved their villages slightly westward just before Jonathan Carver's visit, when he found them on the Fox River. Carver writes in 1766-1768, "On the 25th I arrived at the great town of the Winnebagoes, situated on a small island just

WINNEBAGO MOCCASIN

as you enter the east end of Lake Winnebago. . . . The Winnebagoes can raise about two hundred warriors. Their town contains about fifty houses, which are strongly built with palisades, and the island on which it is situated nearly fifty acres. It lies thirty-five miles, reckoning according to the course of the river, from the Green Bay."

By 1760, after the fall of the French in Canada, the Winnebago gave their loyalty to the British. In the War of 1812 they supported the British cause and helped in the defeat of Michilimackinac, the rapids of the Miami, and the River Raisin. They also allied themselves with other tribes that gathered at Detroit.

WINNEBAGO WARRIOR

In 1806, Zebulon M. Pike says that they lived on the Wisconsin, Rock, and Fox rivers, as well as at the entrance and tip of Green Bay. He estimated there were a total of seven different villages. In 1827 they were battling with the Chippewa and by 1832 they had ceded all their land south of the Wisconsin and Fox rivers, moving to a reservation on the west side of the Mississippi River and north of the Iowa River. In 1832 one of their villages was located at La Crosse, Wisconsin.

Three times the tribe contracted smallpox, and in 1836 more than one-quarter of the Indians perished from this disease which had been brought to this country by the Europeans.

Finally they relinquished all their land east of the Mississippi River, and by 1840 they all had moved farther west to various reservations.

The Winnebago dwellings and dress resembled that of the Sauk and Fox, but they showed individualistic taste in their dress, utensils, and weapons. Their religious values were similar to those of the Central Algonquian tribes and not unlike those of the Dakota and Ponca who were of Siouan stock. The Winnebago's leading deity was known as *Earth-Maker,* and was similar to Gitchi Manito ("Great Spirit," or more precisely, "the mysterious and unknown powers of life that abound in the universe") of the Central Algonquians.

In 1806 their population was estimated to be 1,750 and in 1820 was 5,800. In the years 1837 and 1843 their number was estimated to be about 4,500 souls.

BIBLIOGRAPHY

Blair, Emma Helen. *The Indian Tribes of the Upper Mississippi Valley and Region of the Great Lakes*. Cleveland: The Arthur H. Clark Co., 1911.

Bradley, A. G. *The Fight with France for North America*. New York: E. P. Dutton & Co., 1900.

Callender, C. *Social Organization of the Central Algonkian Indians*. Anthropology Publication No. 7. Milwaukee: Milwaukee Public Museum Publications, 1962.

Carver, Jonathan. *Travels through the Interior Parts of North America*. Reprinted from the 1781 edition. Minneapolis: Ross & Haines, Inc., 1956.

Catlin, George. *Letters and Notes on the North American Indians*. Reprinted from the 1841 edition. Minneapolis: Ross & Haines, Inc., 1965.

Champlain, Samuel de. *Voyages and Discoveries, Made in New France, from the Year 1615 to the End of the Year 1618*. Translated and edited by H. H. Langton and W. F. Ganong. Toronto: The Champlain Society, 1929.

Chard, C. S. "Routes to the Bering Strait." *American Antiquity*. 26: 283-285.

Chesnel, Paul. *History of Cavelier de La Salle, 1643-1687*. New York: G. P. Putnam's Sons, 1932.

Cohen, Hennig and Ward, John William. *The Indian and the White Man*. New York: Doubleday & Co., Inc., 1964.

Colden, C. *The History of the Five Nations Depending on the Province of New York*. Ithaca: Cornell University Press, 1958.

Davis, Emily C. *Ancient Americans*. New York: Henry Holt & Co., 1931.

Deale, V. B. "The History of the Potawotamies before 1722." *Ethnohistory*, 5:305-360.

Densmore, F. *Chippewa Customs*. Bureau of American Ethnology, Bulletin No. 86. Washington: Government Printing Office.

Deuel, Thorne. *American Indian Ways of Life*. Springfield: Illinois State Museum Publications, 1958.

Driver, H. E. *Indians of North America*. Chicago: University of Chicago Press, 1961.

Edmonds, Walter D. *The Musket and the Cross*. Boston: Little, Brown & Co., 1968.

Griffin, J. B. *Lake Superior Copper and the Indians*. Anthropological Papers, No. 17. Museum of Anthropology, University of Michigan. Ann Arbor: University of Michigan Press, 1961.

Hagan, W. T. *The Sac and Fox Indians*. Norman: University of Oklahoma Press, 1958.

Heckewelder, J. G. E. "An Account of the History, Manners and Customs of the Indian Nations, who once Inhabited Pennsylvania and the Neighboring States." *Transactions of the Historical and Literacy Committee of the American Philosophical Society*, 1:1-340.

Hennepin, Louis. *A New Discovery of a Vast Country in America*. 2 vols. Edited by Reuben Gold Thwaites. Elk Grove: A. C. McClurg & Co., 1903.

Hodge, F. W. *Handbook of American Indians North of Mexico*. Bureau of American Ethnology Bulletin No. 30, vols. Smithsonian Institution. Washington: Government Printing Office, 1907-1910.

Hoffman, W. J. "The Menomini Indians." *Annual Report of the Bureau of American Ethnology.* 14:11-328.

Holand, Hjalmer R. *Explorations in America before Columbus.* New York: Twayne Publishers, Inc., 1956.

Irving, John Treat. *Indian Sketches.* Reprinted from the 1888 edition. Edited by J. F. McDermott. Norman: University of Oklahoma Press.

Jenness, D. *The Indians of Canada.* Canada Department of Mines, Bulletin No. 65, 3rd ed. Ottawa: National Museum of Canada, 1955.

Jones, W. *Ethnography of the Fox Indians.* Bureau of American Ethnology, Bulletin 125. Smithsonian Institution. Washington: U.S. Government Printing Office, 1939.

Josephy, Alvin M., ed. *The American Heritage Book of Indians.* New York: American Heritage Publishing Co., 1961.

Karpinski, Louis C. *Bibliography of the Printed Maps of Michigan, 1804-1808.* Lansing: Michigan Historical Commission, 1931.

Kenton, Edna, ed. *The Jesuit Relations and Allied Documents.* New York: The Vanguard Press, 1954.

Kinietz, W. V. "The Indian Tribes of the Western Great Lakes." *Occasional Contributions from the Museum of Anthropology of the University of Michigan,* 10:161-225.

Kohl, Johan G. *Kitchi-Gami.* Minneapolis: Ross & Haines, Inc., 1860.

Lorant, Stefan, ed. *The New World, The First Pictures of America.* New York: Duell, Sloan and Pearce, 1965.

Lossing, Benson J., ed. *Harper's Encyclopaedia of United States History.* 10 vols. New York: Harper & Brothers, 1912.

McKenney, Thomas L. *Sketches of a Tour to the Lakes.* Reprinted from the 1827 edition. Minneapolis: Ross & Haines, 1959.

Martin, P. S., Quimby, G. I., and Collier, D. *Indians before Columbus.* Chicago: University of Chicago Press, 1947.

Michigan Pioneer and Historical Collections, 1874-1929. 40 vols. Lansing: Michigan Historical Commission.

Murray, Hugh. *British America.* 2 vols. Berkshire, England: The Bradley Co., 1840.

Parkman, Francis. *The Conspiracy of Pontiac.* 2 vols. Boston: Little, Brown & Co., 1909.

———— *Count Frontenac and New France under Louis XIV.* Boston: Little, Brown & Co., 1909.

———— A *Half-Century of Conflict.* 2 vols. Boston: Little, Brown & Co., 1912.

———— *The Jesuits in North America in the Seventeenth Century.* Boston: Little, Brown & Co., 1912.

———— *The Journals of Francis Parkman.* 2 vols. Edited by Mason Wade. New York: Harper & Brothers, 1947.

———— *La Salle and the Discovery of the Great West.* Boston: Little Brown & Co., 1910.

———— *The Old Regime in Canada.* Boston: Little, Brown & Co., 1911.

———— *Pioneers of France in the New World.* Boston: Little, Brown & Co., 1912

Quaife, Milo Milton, ed. *The Western Country in the 17th Century, The Memoirs of Lamothe Cadillac and Piere Piette.* Gloucester: Peter Smith, 1947.

Quimby, G. I. *Indian Life in the Upper Great Lakes: 11,000 B.C. to 1800 A.D.* Chicago: University of Chicago Press, 1960.

Radin, Paul. *The Story of the American Indian.* New York: Liveright Publishing Corp., 1944.

———— *Winnebago Culture as Described by Themselves.* Memoirs of the International Journal of American Linguistics. Bloomington: Indiana University, 1950.

Radisson, Peter Esprit. *Voyages of Peter Esprit Radisson, 1652 to 1684.* The Prince Society, 1885.

Raphael, Ralph B. *The Book of American Indians.* New York: Arco Publishing Co., Inc., 1954.

Reid, W. Max. *Lake George and Lake Champlain.* New York: G. P. Putnam's Sons, 1910.

Repplier, Agnes. *Pere Marquette.* Garden City: Doubleday & Co., Inc., 1929.

Ritzenthaler, R. E. "The Oneida Indians of Wisconsin." Bulletins of the Public Museum of the City of Milwaukee, 1950.

———— "The Potawotami Indians of Wisconsin." Bulletins of the Public Museum of the City of Milwaukee, 1953.

———— "Prehistoric Indians of Wisconsin." Bulletins of the Public Museum of the City of Milwaukee, 1967.

———— and Peterson, F. A. "The Mexican Kickapoo Indians." Publications in Anthropology of the Public Museum of the City of Milwaukee, 1956.

Sagard, T. "The Long Journey to the Country of the Hurons." *Publications of the Champlain Society,* 15:1-411.

Schoolcraft, H. R. *Information Respecting the History, Condition and Prospects of the Indian Tribes of the United States.* Philadelphia: J. B. Lippincott & Co., 1853-1856.

Silverberg, J. "The Kickapoo Indians." *Wisconsin Archaeologist,* 38:61-181.

Skinner, A. "The Mascoutens or Prairie Potawotami Indians." Bulletins of the Public Museum of the City of Milwaukee, 1924-1927.

———— "Material Culture of the Menomini. Heye Foundation. Indian Notes and Monographs, Museum of the American Indian, 20, 1921.

———— "Observations of the Ethnology of the Sauk Indians." Bulletins of the Public Museum of the City of Milwaukee, 1923-1925.

Speck, F. G. "The Iroquois." Bulletin No. 23. Cranbrook Institute of Science, 23:1-94.

Swanton, J. R. *The Indian Tribes of North America.* Bureau of American Ethnology, No. 145. Smithsonian Institution. Washington: U.S. Government Printing Office, 1952.

Thwaites, R. G. *The Jesuit Relations and Allied Documents, Travels and Explorations of the Jesuit Missionaries in New France.* 73 vols. Cleveland: Burrows Brothers Co., 1896-1901.

Tooker, Elisabeth. *An Ethnography of the Huron Indians,* 1615-1649. Bureau of American Ethnology Bulletin, No. 190. Washington: U.S. Government Printing Office, 1964.

Verrill, A. Hyatt. *The Real Americans.* New York: G. P. Putnam's Sons, 1954.

Wallace, A. F. *The Modal Personality of the Tuscarora Indians.* Bureau of American Ethnology, Bulletin 150. Washington: U.S. Government Printing Office, 1951.

Wissler, C. *The American Indian.* New York: The Macmillan Co., 1938.

———— *Indians of the United States.* Garden City: Doubleday & Co., Inc., 1948.

LIST OF ILLUSTRATIONS

INDEX OF INDIAN TRIBAL NAMES

248

GENERAL INDEX

Page numbers for paintings and drawings are in italics. A page number followed by the letter m *in parentheses indicates reference to a map.*

250

252

254